I0521753

Ideas in History

Journal of the Nordic Society
for the History of Ideas

Volume 8, no. 1

2014

Museum Tusculanum Press
University of Copenhagen

Ideas in History
Journal of the Nordic Society for the History of Ideas
© 2014 Museum Tusculanum Press, Copenhagen
Composition and cover design: Erling Lynder
ISBN 978 87 635 4292 0
ISSN 1890 1832

Editorial Board
Ingrid Markussen (University of Oslo), Victoria Höög (Lund University), Johan Strang (University of Helsinki), Rebecka Lettevall (Södertörn University), Katarina Leppänen (University of Gothenburg)

About the Journal
Ideas in History is the result of collaborative efforts among nearly a dozen universities and colleges throughout the Nordic countries. The purpose of these initiatives is to further awareness of research, resources and activities in the field of intellectual history in the Nordic countries as well as internationally. The journal aims to create a meeting ground for the study of ideas in historical context across disciplinary, geographical and institutional boundaries. *Ideas in History* welcomes interdisciplinary approaches to intellectual history at the same time it acknowledges specific traditions in the field. *Ideas in History* seeks a pluralism of methodological approaches to intellectual history: reflections on the field, historical contexts studied, subject matter for intellectual-historical investigation, critical understandings of relations between the intellectual past and present as well as the comprehension of culturally, politically and geographically diverse intellectual traditions.

Acknowledgements
Ideas in History is published with the financial assistance of the Nordic Board for Periodicals in the Humanities in the Humanities and Social Sciences.

Manuscripts
Ben Dorfman, Ideas in History
Dept. of Culture and Global Studies Aalborg University
Kroghstræde 3
DK-9220 Aalborg East, Denmark
Email ideasinhistoryjournal@gmail.com

Subscription
Museum Tusculanum Press
University of Copenhagen
Birketinget 6
DK-2300 Copenhagen S, Denmark
Tel. +45 32 34 14 14 / Fax +45 32 58 14 88
Email order@mtp.dk / www.mtp.dk

Contents

Kurt Goldstein's Theory of the Organism and Self-Preservation through Distancing in Twentieth-Century Philosophical Anthropology

*Torbjörn Gustafsson Chorell**

Abstract

Self-preservation is usually associated with the idea of an instinct or a drive to protect living beings from danger. With the aid of the works of the German neurologist Kurt Goldstein, I argue that another concept of self-preservation took shape during the twentieth century. Self-preservation through distancing was not preservation with the aid of a drive or an instinct with a basis in the workings of matter, but a specifically human way of solving the problem of survival. By comparing Goldstein with Arnold Gehlen, Hannah Arendt and Hans Blumenberg, this concept of self-preservation will be shown to have had a more central position in twentieth century intellectual history than generally thought.

Introduction

Studies devoted to the history of the idea of self-preservation have mainly focused on the transition from pre-modern to modern times, from the stoic idea of *oikeiosis*—the self-love of the living thing to remain a unified entity—to self-preservation's association with modern science during the seventeenth century (Engberg-Pedersen 1990; Mulsow 1995, 393–406; Mulsow 1998; Ebeling 1976; Müller 2008). In the seventeenth century, self-preservation was grounded in the law inertia; the most fundamental principle of physical nature. Self-preservation became a problem that had to be solved without relying on external forces or the work of God. The same applied when, during the nineteenth century, self-preservation was connected to models of instincts and drives (Bienenstock 2002). Even conceived of as a drive, however—the force behind animal and potentially human behavior—it was tied to the working of matter. Such reductionism was obvious in the physiologist

* Torbjörn Gustafson Chorell is associate professor of intellectual history and history of science in the Department of History of Science and Ideas at Uppsala Unviersity. This work was supported by the Swedish Research Council.

and Nobel Prize laureate C. S. Sherrington's analysis of the organism in the 1930s.

> The individual life in virtue of its mind uses strategy to promote life and that of its seed, and strategy to avoid death. To the unconscious "urge-to-live" is added conscious "zest-to-live." It is life which *would* live. The "conservation of self" is, Dr. Charles Myers tells us, a principle in psychology as real and important as the physicists' principle of "conservation of energy." (Sherrington 1942, 378–379)

Nonetheless, there is another concept of self-preservation at work during the twentieth century. Self-preservation through distancing was not preservation with the aid of a drive or an instinct with a basis in the working of matter. Rather, it was a specifically human way of solving the problem of survival. This idea of self-preservation was upheld in opposition to theories of human behavior emanating from the sciences, especially evolutionary theory. I will analyze this new concept of self-preservation with the aid of the German neurologist Kurt Goldstein. Out of his work with patients with severe brain damage both during and after the First World War, Goldstein developed an anthropology which took its point of departure from criticism of the old idea of self-preservation. By focusing on his idea of human existence, I want to give an outline of this yet underexplored notion of self-preservation in twentieth-century intellectual history and the specific kind of humanism to which it gave rise. Human language, imagination, technical skills, and reason were examples of tools that maintained distance from nature and helped human-ity to create a world that functioned as its own habitat. The manmade world was what protected human beings from that which would destroy them if they ventured beyond a safe distance.

Goldstein, born into a Jewish family in Katowice, Germany (now Poland) in 1878 (he died in America in 1965) has been neglected by intellectual his-torians and historians of medicine despite his place in some of the intense debates among intellectuals of his generation. This includes the influence he exerted on thinkers such as Ernst Cassirer (his cousin), Georges Canguilhem and Maurice Merleau-Ponty (Harrington 1996, 148–49, 158). Goldstein is only mentioned in passing in Joachim Fischer's (2008) analysis of the surpris-ingly neglected paradigm, as he calls it, of German philosophical anthropol-ogy. The point of departure for this paradigm was the way in which living things encountered and handled their environments. The systematic study of forms of life revealed how humans had created a specific way of solving problems. Although Goldstein might not meet all the criteria of this paradigm, as outlined by Fischer (Fischer 2009, 154–163), he did have many affinities with the philosophy which took shape in the works of Helmut Plessner and Max Scheler in the 1920s. The concept of self-preservation I am interested in had particular resonance among the philosophical anthropologists Fischer highlights. Anne Harrington devotes a chapter to Goldstein in her book on holism in early twentieth-century science (Harrington 1996, 140–174), and his place in the history of phenomenology was discussed by Herbert Spiegelberg (1972, 301–318). Goldstein also appears in histories of aphasia and other language disturbances, for instance in L.S. Jacyna's book on narrative language and the brain (2000, 225–230). Nonetheless, his own output in works like *Der Aufbau des Organismus* (1934), which was written during intense months in the Netherlands after he fled Germany after a brutal encounter with the Gestapo, and *Human Nature in the Light of Psychopathology* (1940), which was the outcome of a lecture series at American universities, and other works that retrospectively used the experiences from the twenties and the First World War deserves more attention than they have received so far. However, the main reason for choosing Goldstein as a center of analysis is to show how the idea of self-preservation, which has been so central to modern intellectual history in ethics, psychology and natural philosophy, in his work gained decisively new figurations. The consequences of this demand further analysis.

Self-Preservation and Self-Actualization
One can see how this new figuration takes shape in Goldstein's medical treatises and methodological works. In common with many others during the inter-war period, he perceived that there was a crisis in the understanding of human existence. For Goldstein, this was due to human beings having a "false idea" of their own nature (Goldstein 1940, 7). "False idea" emanated from Goldstein's opinion that mankind based the understanding of itself on a wrong conception of human drives. This especially concerned the drive to preserve oneself. The self-preservation of living organisms, and, in particular, that of *Homo sapiens*, was not a problem solved by referring to instincts or drives, Goldstein argued in *Der Aufbau des Organismus*. Theories based on the existence of reflexes, instincts, and drives originated in observations of maturing children and animals that merely reacted to dangerous situations when they were subjected to laboratory experiments:

Frequently, the law of maintaining the existent state—the self-preservation—is considered as the basic law of life. I believe such a concept could arise only because one had assumed, as a starting point, the experiences in abnormal conditions or experimental situations. The tendency to maintain the existent state is characteristic for sick people and is a sign of anomalous life, a decay of life. The tendency of normal life is toward activity and progress. For the sick, the only form of self-actualization that remains is the maintenance of the existent state (Goldstein 2000, 162)

The common idea of self-preservation was, Goldstein argues, modeled on the law of inertia as a matter of maintaining the existing state. According to him, this conception was part of a general misunderstanding about the behaviour of organisms. If one realized that the only goal of the organism was to actualize its own nature, this would answer many questions. If, for example, a sick or injured organism could not regain its former capacity, it, nonetheless, sought to actualize itself as much as possible. "This tendency to actualize its nature, to actualize 'itself', is the basic drive, the only drive by which the life of the organism is determined" (Goldstein 2000, 162).

The thesis that organisms strive to actualize their nature resembles a biological version of the idea of *Bildung*. In the striving toward self-actualization, the organism constantly encountered obstacles that it had to overcome. Illnesses and injuries could be such obstacles. This was the case in the cases that Goldstein and the psychologist Adhémar Gelb studied at the Frankfurt Neurological Institute where, during the 1920s, they had cared for and studied patients who had suffered severe skull injuries. According to Goldstein's own estimation, he had systematically studied about two thousand patients, some of them for as long as a decade (Goldstein 1942, 15–20). Every injury or illness should be viewed as a more or less brutal collision with the environment. In extreme cases, injuries or illnesses were equivalent to the kind of situation an animal found itself in when it was subjected to physiological experiments. The goal was that the imbalance caused by the illness or the injury had to be eliminated, as the organism would perish were this not done. As the above quote indicates, self-preservation as maintenance of the existing state was the only means the organism had at its disposal for actualizing itself in these particular situations. When complex organisms were trying to preserve themselves, for example with automatic performances, it was a sign of decay of life or "a symptom of abnormality." "Preservation of material existence becomes 'essential' only after defect sets in, and possibly in certain emergencies" (Goldstein 2000, 47).

It may appear from the evidence presented to this point that Goldstein dismissed the striving towards self-preservation as merely a phenomenon that appeared in cases of pathology. However, that would be to interpret him too hastily. Although he nowhere writes about it explicitly, it can be reconstructed from his overall conception of the sick and healthy organism that self-preservation had to be understood as a distancing from the kinds of situations that would prevent the organism's actualization of its capacities.

Self-Preservation through Distancing
To reconstruct Goldstein's idea of self-preservation, one can start with one of his key concepts: catastrophic reaction. Organisms confronted with situations that they could not master reacted with anxiety. Like the philosophers and theologians who also used this concept, anxiety was denoted by Goldstein as the subjective side of the objective fact that the organism faced situations that it could not overcome; anxiety was a blank terror when encountering an undefined object. For the severely injured or sick individual, even straightforward situations represented insurmountable obstacles and resulted in anxiety reactions (Goldstein 1940, 90). Anxiety thus differed from fear, which always related to specific objects.

The consequence of this was that anxiety was a basic condition of human nature (Goldstein 1971a). It was, therefore, essential for sick individuals to adapt their lifestyle so that situations that caused catastrophic reactions did not need to occur. This manifested itself in sick and injured individuals voluntary withdrawal from the surrounding environment and their isolating themselves, or arranging their existence so meticulously that they could assert control of the environment. This manifested itself in passivity and in simply not reacting to what was happening around them. It also manifested itself in frenetic activity involving things that the individual could handle (Goldstein 1940, 95–108). By contrast, healthy organisms reacted creatively to the demands of their milieu. The concept of health incorporated the notion that organisms could adapt and thereby grow: "an organism is normal and healthy when its tendency toward self-actualization issues from within, and when it overcomes the disturbance arising from its clash with the world not by virtue of anxiety but through the joy of coming to terms with the world," wrote Goldstein (1940, 112). Joy was the feeling of the healthy organism in the face of the challenges of its existence. Joy was not the same as pleasure. According to Goldstein, pleasure was the static feeling that sick individuals experienced when their suffering was temporarily mitigated (Goldstein 1971b, 437–438; Goldstein 1970, 182).

Goldstein's concept of health was thus, not based on the idea that regaining one's health after an illness was a return to a pre-illness state. Regaining health rather represented the establishment of a new order responding to the organism's ability to actualize its nature by creating a new living environment for itself. The basic perspective on the relationship between the organism and its environment was that of the biologist Jacob von Uexküll: "Each organism has its milieu … its existence and its 'normal' performances are dependent on the condition that a state of adaptation can come about between its structure and the environmental events, allowing the formation of an 'adequate' milieu" (Goldstein 2000, 106) According to Uexküll, the organism's relation to its milieu should not be understood as that of a subject's relation to an object, but rather as a reciprocal creation. The living environment is created by an organism, which is shaped by the milieu that it can produce. This means that every species and every individual lives in a unique, self-contained environment. The fox lives in a fox world, the crow in a crow world. Every animal creates the environment it requires for its needs. When organisms need change, the environment also changes. A completely integrated relationship between the subject and its milieu is the outcome. It was this interaction researchers should study (Harrington 1996, 34–48; Feuerhahn 2009). When applied to Goldstein's analysis of the meaning of health and illness, this notion meant that the patients regained their health when they succeeded in creating a new milieu for themselves, or as he preferred to phrase it: "The changed organism must find, in the 'world', a new 'milieu'" (Goldstein 2000, 337, 388). The terms world and milieu are evasive in Goldstein's works. They must be viewed in the light of the philosophical tradition that he shared with such thinkers as Max Scheler and Ernst Cassirer. The animals had a natural environment, while human beings also had a world which protected them from a direct encounter with nature. Within this human world, the sick or injured individual had to create his or her own milieu so as to avoid encountering situations that could not be mastered.

The concept was clear: to be able to survive, mankind had to trust in its capacity to withdraw and create distance from the dangerous parts of nature that surrounded it by creating a world or habitable milieu within nature. There was a strong moral sense to this ability determining the value of human life itself. Anxiety-ridden situations were something that afflicted all human beings. This reality contained a moral that was crucial to Goldstein's existential perspective. "The capacity for bearing anxiety is the manifestation of genuine courage, in which ultimately one is concerned not with the things of the world but with a threat to existence," Goldstein (1940, 113) argued. How one handles one's own anxiety—here it is inevitable that one associates Goldstein's reflections with his own experiences of persecution and threats—demonstrates the degree of freedom that the individual human being possesses (Goldstein 1940, 114). The condition for the existence of this freedom was, however, the ability to distance oneself to the environment. Without this distance, the individual would fall back into mere survival, and would have lost its (moral) integrity or "Being" (Goldstein 2000, 47).

In *Human Nature in the Light of Psychopathology* (1940), the distinction between an abstract and a concrete attitude was an important feature. Having an abstract attitude meant being able to fundamentally distinguish oneself from the environment that surrounded the individual. It was the abstract attitude that endowed mankind with the ability to create a culture, and in so doing, a world. Language was perhaps the foremost manifestation of the human ability to live in an abstract fashion: "in none of his cultural creations does man reveal himself so fully as in the creation of language itself," wrote Goldstein (1940, 83). Language expressed the human organism's way of coming to terms with the situation it found itself in.

What Goldstein formulated using the concept of abstract attitude could also be formulated with Cassirer's concept of symbolic forms. There had long been a mutual exchange between the two, and during the 1920s when Cassirer was working on *Die Philosophie des symbolischen Formen* (*The Philosophy of Symbolic Forms*) (1924–30), he had often been in contact with his cousin (Harrington 1996, 148–149). Symbolic forms, which, according to Cassirer, expressed the very essence of man, were placed between him and reality in order to create the distance required for the possibility of seeing a verifying reality. Those patients who had been under Goldstein's care lacked the ability to create distance due to the fact that the abstract attitude had vanished or had been severely affected by their injuries. They were more directly at the mercy of their environment (again, perceived as a threat to their existence).

In summary, for Goldstein, self-preservation was not a basic drive or an instinct. The drive to preserve material existence was an expression of pathology and the fact that the organism could not actualize itself in any other way. The normal behavior of the organism presupposed that distance from the environment had been established and maintained. Self-preservation was thus an activity engaged in unreflectively by healthy organisms at all times. In a manner of speaking, in modern societies, the problem of self-preservation had already been solved by the customs and institutions that were products of mankind's creativity and abstract attitude. It was through their ingenuity that human beings had created the culture that afforded them protection and security. In *Human Nature*, Goldstein posed the question of how it came about that cultures took on different forms. "The matter becomes intelligible only if one regards the forms as expressions of the concrete powers of man, and of his tendency to effect a realization of his nature. Only when the world is adequate to man's nature do we find what we call security," he wrote (Goldstein 1940, 111, 216, 219). The human form of life, including the cultures that humans had created for themselves, expressed their self-preservation through a distancing from the nature that would destroy them if they encountered it without the protection of their world.

Man's Vulnerability According to Gehlen

Implicitly, such ideas contained perspectives on mankind's relationship to nature that were also developed, albeit differently, by Arnold Gehlen. Goldstein can be compared with Gehlen; such a comparison will strengthen the argument that the concept of self-preservation through distancing was an important aspect of twentieth-century thought generally. This latter claim will be further supported by other examples in part three.

The same year that Goldstein published his book on human nature in the light of psychopathological illnesses, Gehlen published the first edition of *Der Mensch: Seine Natur und seine Stellung in der Welt* (1940). As a supporter of National Socialism in the 1930s, on which his early career depended, and his later right-wing political stance, in political terms he and the socialist Goldstein were worlds apart. However, their analysis of human beings included several common issues and reference points. Gehlen was also critical of the evolutionary theory of transitions between drives, instincts, and conscious action. Both were skeptical of dualistic theories and made similar criticisms of, for example, Max Scheler's division between life and consciousness (Gehlen 1988, 14–17; Goldstein 2000, 383–385, 353–355). Man, Gehlen wrote, borrowing an observation from Friedrich Nietzsche's *Jenseits von Gut und Böse* (*Beyond Good and Evil*), was the not-yet-determined animal (Gehlen 1988, 4). This meant that man was not fixed in the form of predetermined drives or instincts except during the very first year of life.

Nietzsche's concept of man's indeterminacy made it possible to characterize the human being as a deficient being. This idea had been previously expressed by several people, among them Helmut Plessner and Paul Alsberg in the 1920s, but perhaps no one had done so in such colorful terms as J .G.Herder in his famous late-eighteenth-century analysis of the origin of language. In Gehlen's opinion, anthropology had not progressed much further, even by the middle of the twentieth-century (Gehlen 1988, 76). The human child, Herder wrote (2002, 80–81), is "the most orphaned child of nature." Naked, weak, and unarmed, without tools to ensure its survival, it is born into the world. Humans lacked animal instincts and were not tied to a specific environment. In return, they had obtained freedom, but one that forced them to create their own culture with the aid of their intelligence. Gehlen's anthropology followed the same principles yet was based on the findings from the modern sciences. The point of a philosophical anthropology was formulating principles that applied to the understanding of man and the difference between human living conditions and those of animals. In the case of humans, nature had experimented with an entirely new form of organization. The question was what it comprised.

With the support of contemporary researchers such as Konrad Lorenz, Gehlen argued that human beings lacked fixed instincts and drives They also lacked defense mechanisms and physical strength; they were slow and bad at climbing, their teeth were too weak to process raw food and their skin provided poor protection against heat and cold. Mankind did not have its own natural environment and human beings could live in deserts as well as in rain forests and icy polar regions. Human beings were open to the world (*weltoffen*), as Gehlen wrote using Scheler's and Plessner's term. They thus lacked an external milieu in the way that animals had shaped one for themselves through their interaction with nature (Scheler 1961, 39–40). Gehlen expressed this in terms of human beings having a world to which they related to but no natural environment. Openness to the world also meant that surviving was a problem that man was compelled to solve: "[H]is survival becomes his greatest challenge and greatest accomplishment. Quite simply, it is a considerable feat for Man to survive from one year to the next, and all his abilities are employed toward this end" (Gehlen1988, 10). The environment in which humans found themselves was full of surprises. They were constantly compelled to acquire overview and orientation since they, unlike animals, could not rely on the help of innate instincts that were triggered under specific circumstances. What was innate to animals, mankind had to teach itself. In common with other researchers, Gehlen criticized those who attempted to produce long lists of instincts pertaining to human behavior. Regarding humans, it was more the case that they had a surplus of energy. A creature that lacked fixed behavior patterns and, at the same time, was full of energy that had to be released was, as Carl-Göran Heidegren (2002, 56) expressed it, "unpredictable and unstable." How is all that energy to be channeled?

According to Gehlen, it was essential that human beings educate themselves and devote themselves to exercise. This was necessary based on the conditions of their existence. Were they to abandon self-discipline, then their survival chances would diminish. Self-discipline required the presence of an inner distance between the drives and the actions. Sometimes they had to inhibit the satisfaction that they felt in anticipation of certain acts. At other times, they had to restrain needs and abstain from actions that would give them pleasure. Human beings could either accept or reject their drives. In this way, by shaping themselves, they eventually became a character, i.e. a being that had become predictable precisely because it had learned to pursue certain interests and abstain from others (Gehlen1988, 368–376).

A consequence of saying yes or no to their drives was that human beings gained an inner life that helped them to control and unburden themselves. Unburdening (*Entlastung*) was "the centre and core" of Gehlen's thought, Christian Thies (2007, 105) writes. This unburdening consisted of customs, rituals, and routines, which meant that human beings did not have to think about what they did and demonstrated that their existence was under control. The outcome of this unburdening was that human beings constantly distanced themselves from a direct encounter with nature through their ability to achieve overview and foresee their actions (Gehlen 1988, 59–61). As there was a gulf between their desires and their actions, so there was a chasm between the self and the environment.

In the terms that we have previously used in the analysis of Goldstein, it can be said that human beings were forced to create a world for themselves in the space opened by this chasm. This world made it impossible for them to return to nature. This would be tantamount to subjecting themselves to insurmountable dangers. The answer to the question of how human beings can survive in spite of their underdeveloped instincts and excessive needs was that human beings had to transform their actions and interactions with others into binding structures that they subjected themselves to. A society's institutions gave human beings the direction they lacked, at the same time it provided security in finding their way in the world, (animals were given this by instinct). An institution was thus a response to the problem of man's existence—a way in which human self-preservation was ensured through self-imposed means of orientation and the creation of distance from the environment (Gehlen 1964, 7–121). That was part of humankind's second nature, its self-created culture or world that was essential for its survival. Culture was "man's restructured nature, within which he can survive...the cultural world exists for Man in exactly the same way in which the environment exists for an animal" (Gehlen 1988, 29). The world surrounding human beings bore witness to the fact that they had succeeded well in creating an environment which allowed them to distance themselves from nature.

The affinities between Gehlen and Goldstein are obvious. They both considered mankind in a unique position, leading its life in a fundamentally different manner from animals. Humankind was just as much part of nature as animals, yet lived its life according to other principles. As Goldstein put it, language and the thinking it gave rise to revealed mankind's uniqueness, both in its relationship to the world and in the bonding to its fellow beings. However, language was not just a means of communication or naming of objects. Rather, language represent[ed] a particular way of building up the world." "It would be impossible for animals to create a language, because they do not have this conceptual approach toward the world. If they had, they would be not animals but human beings" (Goldstein 1940, 83). However, a conceptual approach toward the world was already in itself a way of removing oneself from immediate contact with it. The reason for mankind's survival was its capacity to create a physical and mental world and thereby distance from the kinds of things that threatened its existence. This also meant that the creation of the world was a collective effort to protect each other from physical and psychical harm.

In his later texts, Goldstein increasingly stressed the relationship with other individuals as a condition for both self-actualization and self-preservation. The child, he wrote, is born helpless into the world without the abstract attitude required for survival. That the child did not perish was because of innate mechanisms activated at birth as well as due to the fact that other human beings, especially parents, protected it. They used the abstract attitude to create a world for the child that would harmonize with its capacities and maturity, and this recalled to a considerable degree how adults had done for themselves (Goldstein1971c, 466–484). This was not instinctual behavior or a matter of a drive in the organism, but the very activity through which human beings secured their physical existence.

Self-Preservation through Distancing: Arendt and Blumenberg

With these ideas, we have come full circle. This is to the extent that we encounter another concept of self-preservation in Goldstein's theory of the organism. What this concept entailed was no less than a specific kind of humanism that emphasized a human being's unique kind of existence in contrast to evolutionary and other naturalistic or reductionist theories. Mankind did not live the same kind of life as animals. Humanity was not ruled by the same forces that were used to explain animal life in general. At the same time, this perspective did not presuppose a duality or some kind of transcendence of nature. To Goldstein, man's existence was but based on different principles than animal existence. As the physician Paul Alsberg put it in the early 1920s, animals lived under the principle of body-compulsion. Humanity developed along a different route, that of "the principle of body-liberation." "The principle of human evolution is that of freeing Man from the compulsion of body-adaptation by means of artificial tools" (Alsberg1970, 38). Self-preservation could not be understood as a natural drive if mankind's way of living was to be something different from animal life. Distancing was the human mode of self-preservation in the face of a lack of other natural means of survival.[1]

There is, therefore, much to support the thesis that one encounters a new concept of self-preservation during the twentieth century, at least among thinkers associated with German philosophical anthropology. Animals, Erich Rothacker wrote in the 1940s, live in "gelebten Welten" (lived world), an environment they are perfectly adapted to humans live in "erkämpften Welten," worlds won by their struggle to build a world that creates distance from the surroundings (Rothacker 1934, 99–112). Another example is Hannah Arendt. Mankind needed to raise a protective wall between itself and nature, she wrote in *The Human Condition* (1958). This echoes the kind of idea of self-preservation considered here. Without a protecting wall between man and nature, mankind would confront

---

1 A symbolic illustration of this was given by Max Horkheimer and Theodor Adorno, both of whom were familiar with the work of Goldstein, in the retelling of the story of Odysseus' encounter with the sirens in *The Dialectic of Enlightenment* (1943). Horkheimer and Adorno had worked in Adhémar Gelb's, i.e. Kurt Goldstein's colleague's, psychological laboratory in the 1920s (Amidon 2008, 112). Goldstein once published an article in a volume edited by Horkheimer, (Goldstein 1936, 656–668). On Horkheimer, Adorno and self-preservation, see for instance (Stirk 1992) and (Cook 2006, 433–447).

...the sublime indifference of an untouched nature, whose overwhelming elementary force, on the contrary, will compel them to swing relentlessly in the circle of their own biological movement, which fits so closely into the over-all cyclical movement of nature's household. Only we who have erected the objectivity of a world of our own from what nature gives us, who have built it into the environment of nature so that we are protected from her, can look upon nature as something "objective." Without a world between men and nature, there is eternal movement, but no objectivity. (Arendt 1958, 137)

The world created by man himself was his way of creating the necessary distance between himself and nature's "sublime indifference" to human needs. Distancing also meant that nature could, and had to, be dominated and controlled by humans with the aid of the tools they had created and used to shape nature into a habitable place. If man failed to build within nature a world that sheltered him, he would disappear into that nature that existed outside of him.[2]

As a last example, I introduce Hans Blumenberg to whom the principle of self-preservation through distancing defined modernity itself (Schultz 1999, 244–265). Blumenberg's essays and remarks on the principle of self-preservation have been the focus of debate for many years. But introducing him also makes it possible to imagine, as Peter E. Gordon (2014, 44) put it, "that ideas from the past might still be available for *critical appropriation in the present.*" Introducing Blumenberg as an example of the way self-preservation through distancing has been reproduced in the present carries, therefore, theoretical implications. Ideas are legitimate objects of study even if they are not primarily analyzed within a circumscribed temporal and spatial context.

---

2 In *The Origins of Totalitarianism* (1951), the idea of nature's indifference to man's disappearance appeared in a slightly different way: "no longer separated by space and nature and, consequently, by spiritually insurmountable walls of history and culture, mankind will either find a way to live in and rule together an overcrowded earth or it will perish – an event which will leave the sublime indifference of nature untouched" (Arendt 1951, 436). An interesting article in this respect is Mayor (1979, 131–155), who reads her in the light of German philosophical anthropology, especially Helmut Plessner. To make self-preservation into the most basic drive of animal and human behavior, Arendt wrote in *Life of the Mind*, was a way of maintaining a unified worldview. Referring to the Swiss zoologist Adolf Portmann, she spoke of an ever present "urge to appear" (Arendt 1978, 26–28). Portmann was also referred to by Gehlen who used his theory that man was born too early and that her first year of living was to be seen as an extra-uterus year outside of the mother's body. On Portmann's place within German philosophical anthropology, see Fischer (2008, 197–205, 239–242).

Blumenberg argued that it seemed as though human beings prior to the modern era did not really comprehend that there were insufficient assets to meet their needs. To them, the problem seemed to be the imbalanced distribution of the assets. The arrival of modernity brought a change. This was in the sense that human beings felt that they always had too little. Self-preservation was removed from the biological realm where it had led an invisible existence and became part of human self-understanding. To rely on nature or providence having arranged everything for the best was insufficient. It was now a matter of organizing existence so that man could preserve himself. The interest in finding technical solutions to problems was a response to the need for protection that man's new understanding of his relationship with nature had brought about. However, in contrast to this loss of belief that creation has been undertaken to specifically suit human needs, Blumenberg formulated self-assertion as an existential program of artful mastery of a world (Blumenberg 1983, 138).

Self-assertion was self-preserving in that it was an active means of creating the distance required in order for man to have a habitable world. Drawing on Nietzsche's critique of teleology, Blumenberg distinguished self-assertion from biological self-preservation. For Nietzsche, self-preservation was a result of the will to power. Self-preservation could, therefore, not be an innate drive, but was rather a reaction to an environment that was considered to be indifferent to man's needs (Nietzsche 2002, I: 13). We can easily see how this Nietzschean argument also applies to Goldstein's critique of the concept of self-preservation and is echoed in Blumenberg's historicisation of the idea of self-preservation.

For Blumenberg, there was a fundamental difference between the concept of self-preservation developed by the Stoics (*oikeoisis*, a basic self-love of one's integrity) and that which characterized modern times. Its beginning could be traced to the ideas of late Scholasticism about a constantly ongoing creation (Dilthey 1914, 283–296). In this theological context, all creatures were dependent on God's continuous efforts to maintain his creation. During the 1600s, according to Blumenberg, self-preservation came to be linked to the law of inertia—that everything remains in the same state until something disturbs it. Preservation was thus no longer dependent on the existence of an external power that guaranteed existence. Self-preservation was rather linked to reason's way of organizing existence, as in the case of Thomas Hobbes. "The passage beyond the state of nature in the contract of submission no longer admits of comparison with an act of self-preservation on impulse ... it is rational behavior as an act which must not come into conflict with the preservation of mere existence, existence being a condition of acting," Blumenberg (1983a, 219) argued.[3] In the modern era, self-preservation was part of reason itself; self-preservation was a tool for the conduct that led to man distancing himself from nature as well as for organizing social intercourse with other humans (Klein 2009, 165–181).

As the examples of Goldstein and Gehlen demonstrate, and Arendt and Blumenberg confirm, the problem of human self-preservation was solved not by recourse to a theory of drives but as a belief that human existence demanded the creation of a habitable world within nature that distanced mankind from whatever life-threatening entities it would encounter if this distance, world or shield was not in place. This was the case regardless of whether one was talking about man's ontology (as in the case of Blumenberg's concept of the "absoluteness of reality" (Wetz 2009, 389–414), society or the way the body reacted to severe injuries. The principle of self-preservation through distancing was everywhere active. It was presupposed by Goldstein in the 1930s:

[T]he normal organism is characterized as a 'Being' in a temporal succession of definite form. For the realization of this 'Being', the existence, the 'mere being alive', plays, of course, a prominent but by no means *the* essential role. Under extreme circumstances, it can be compatible with the 'nature' of an organism to renounce life, that is give up its bodily existence, in order to save its most essential characteristics—for example, a man's ethical convictions. Preservation of material existence becomes 'essential' only after the defect sets in, and possibly in certain emergencies. (Goldstein 2000, 47)

Only in extreme circumstances, when the distance from reality or the surrounding nature was blocked, self-preservation manifested itself as a drive for survival. The normal and healthy organism had another relation to nature

---

3 Hans Blumenberg's interpretation drew attention from philosophers and theologians who criticized it on the ground that self-preservation presupposed the existence of consciousness and therefore could not be grounded in physical laws of nature. According to Dieter Henrich, whose critique was echoed in the works of Wolfgang Pannenberg, self-preservation assumed that the self was dependent on something outside itself. The perfect control and basis in itself that the concept of self-preservation implied were lacking. Similarly, self-preservation presupposed self-consciousness, which meant that the connection with the law of inertia could not be self-evident. That everything preserves its condition does not mean that everything has a principle of self-preservation since the existence of a self requires consciousness; see (Henrich 1976, 11, 123–143) and (Pannenberg 1990, 62–65) and (Pannenberg 1994, 33, 51–52).

that made it possible to act in different ways. Even highly valued moral and religious actions such as self-sacrifice were only possible in situations where the protecting world was in place. The act of sacrificing oneself presupposed that acute needs for survival had been realized and that the abstract attitude, and thereby distance from nature was in place. Thus, when Blumenberg, in a posthumous work, answered the question as to how man's existence was possible "through a kind of distance" he confirmed a concept of self-preservation that had been playing a central role in philosophical thinking for almost a century (Blumenberg 2006, 570, 585).

References

Alsberg, Paul. 1970. *In Quest of Man: A Biological Approach to the Problem of Man's Place in Nature.* Oxford and New York: Pergamon Press.

Amidon, Kevin S. 2008. "'Diesmal fehlt die Biologie!' Max Horkheimer, Richard Thunwald, and the Biological Prehistory of German *Sozialforschung.*" *New German Critique* 104: 103–137.

Arendt, Hannah. 1951. *The Origins of Totalitarianism.* New York: Harcourt Press.

———. 1958. *The Human Condition.* Chicago: University of Chicago Press.

———. 1978. *Life of the Mind,* vol. 1. New York: Secker & Warburg.

Bienenstock, Myriam. 2002. "Trieb, Tendence, Instinct, Pulsion." *Revue Germanique Internationale* 18. Paris: Presses Universitaires de France.

Blumenberg, Hans. 1983. *The Legitimacy of the Modern Age.* Cambridge, MA: The MIT Press.

———. 1983a. "Self-Preservation and Inertia: On the Constitution of Modern Rationality." *Contemporary German Philosophy* 3: 209–256.

———. 2006. *Beschreibung des Menschen.* Edited by Manfred Sommer. Frankfurt am Main: Suhrkamp Verlag.

Cook, Deborah. 2006. "Staying Alive: Adorno and Habermas on Self-Preservation and Late Capitalism." *Rethinking Marxism* 18(3): 433–437.

Dilthey, Wilhelm. 1914. *Weltanschauung und Analyse des Menschen seit Renaissance und Reformation.* Gesammelte Schriften 2. Leipzig and Berlin: Verlag B.G. Teuber.

Ebeling, Hans, ed. 1976. *Subjektivität und Selbsterhaltung: Beiträge zur Diagnose der Moderne.* Frankfurt am Main: Suhrkamp.

Engberg-Pedersen, Troels. 1990. *The Stoic Theory of Oikeiosis: Moral Development and Social Interaction in Early Stoic Philosophy.* Aarhus: Aarhus University Press.

Feuerbahn, Wolf. 2009. "Du milieu à l'*Umwelt*: Enjeux d'un changement terminologique." *Revue philosophique de la France et de l'Étranger* 199(4): 419–438.

Fischer, Joachim. 2008. *Philosophische Anthropologie: Eine Denkrichtung 20. Jahrhundert.* Freiburg and Munich: Verlag Karl Alber.

———. 2009. "Exploring the Core Identity of Philosophical Anthropology through the Works of Max Scheler, Helmuth Plessner, and Arnold Gehlen." *Iris* 1(2): 153–170.

Gehlen, Arnold. 1964. *Urmensch und Spätkultur: Philosophische Ergebnisse und Aussagen,* 2nd ed. Frankfurt am Main & Bonn: Althenäum Verlag.

———. 1988. *Man: His Nature and Place in the World.* Translated by Clare McMillan and Karl Pillemer. New York: Columbia University Press.

Goldstein, Kurt. 1936. "Bemerkungen über die Bedeutung der Biologie für die Soziologie anlässlich des Autoritätsproblem." In *Studien über Autorität und Familie*, edited by Max Horkheimer. Paris: Félix Alcan.

———. 1940. *Human Nature in the Light of Psychopathology.* Cambridge, MA: Harvard University Press.

———. 1942. *After-Effects of Brain of Brain Injuries in War: Their Evaluation and Treatment: The Application of Psychological Methods in the Clinic.* London: William Heinemann.

———. 1970. "Health as Value." *New Knowledge in Human Values*, edited by Abraham H. Maslow. Chicago: Gateway.

———. 1971a. "Zur Problem der Angst." In *Selected Papers/Ausgewälte Schriften*, edited by Aron Gurwitch, Elise M. Goldstein Haudek and William E. Haudek, 231–262. The Hague: Martinus Nijhoff.

———. 1971b. "On Emotions: Considerations from the Organismic Point of View." In *Selected Papers/Ausgewälte Schriften*, edited by Aron Gurwitch, Elise M. Goldstein Haudek and William E. Haudek, 425–438. The Hague: Martinus Nijhoff. Originally published in *Journal of Psychology* 31, 1951, 37–49.

———. 1971c. "The Smiling of the Infant and the problem of Understanding the Other." In *Selected Papers/Ausgewälte Schriften*, edited by Aron Gurwitch, Elise M. Goldstein Haudek and William E. Haudek, 466–484. The Hague: Martinus Nijhoff.

———. 2000. *The Organism: A Holistic Approach to Biology Derived from Pathological Data in Man.* New York: Zone Books.

Gordon, Peter E. 2014. "Contextualism and Criticism in the History of Ideas." In *Rethinking Modern European Intellectual History*, edited by Darrin H. McMahon and Samuel Moys, 32–55. Oxford: Oxford University Press.

Harrington, Anne. 1996. *Reenchanted Science: Holism in German Culture from Wilhelm II to Hitler.* Princeton: Princeton University Press.

Heidegren, Carl-Göran. 2002. *Antropologi, samhällsteori och politik: Radikalkonservatism och kritisk teori.* Göteborg: Daidalos.

Henrich, Dieter. 1976. "Die Grundstruktur der modernen Philosophie." In *Subjektivität und Selbsterhaltung: Beiträge zur Diagnose der* Moderne, edited by Hans Ebeling, 97–121.Frankfurt am Main: Suhrkamp.

Heinrich, Dieter. 1976a. "Über Selbstbewusstsein und Selbsterhaltung."In *Subjektivität und Selbsterhaltung: Beiträge zur Diagnose der Moderne*, edited by Hans Ebeling, 122–143. Frankfurt am Main: Suhrkamp.

Herder, J.G. 2002. *Philosophical Writings.* Edited and translated by Michael N. Forster. Cambridge: Cambridge University Press.

Jacyna, L.S. 2000. *Lost Words: Narratives of Language and the Brain 1825–1925*. Princeton: Princeton University Press.

Klein, Rebekka. 2009. "Das Ende der Humanevolution? Blumenbergs Argumente gegen einem Erklärungsprimat von Darwin's Evolutionstheori." In *Auf Distanz zur Natur: Philosophische und theologische Perspektiven in Hans Blumenbergs Anthropologie*, edited by Rebekka Klein, 165–181. Würzburg: Königshausen & Neumann.

Mayor, Robert W. 1979. "A Reading of Hannah Arendt's 'Unusual' Distinction between Labor and Work." In *Hannah Arendt: The Recovery of the Public World*, edited by Melvyn A. Hill. New York: St. Martin's Press.

Mulsow, Martin. 1995. "Selbsterhaltung." *Historische Wörterbuch der Philosophie*, vol. 9, edited by Joachim Ritter and Karlfried Gründer, 393–406. Basel: Schwabe AG Verlag.

———. 1998. *Frühneuzeitliche Selbsterhaltung: Telesio und die Naturphilophie der Renaissance*. Tübingen: Niemeyer.

Müller, Klaus. 2008. "Selbsterhaltung: Ein stoisches Korrektur spätmoderner Kritik am modernen Subjektgedanken." In *Von Selbst-Verständnis in Antike und Neuzeit/Notions of the Self in Antiquity and Beyond*, edited by Alexander Arweiler & Melanie Möller, 381–395. Berlin and New York: Walter de Gruyter.

Nietzsche, Friedrich. 2002. *Beyond Good and Evil: Prelude to a Philosophy of the Future*. Edited by Rolf-Peter Horstmann and Judith Norman. Translated by Judith Norman. Cambridge: Cambridge University Press.

Pannenberg, Wolfgang. 1990. *Metaphysics and the Idea of God*. Translated by Philip Clayton. Edinburgh: T & T Clark.

———. 1994. *Systematic Theology*, vol. 2. Translated by Geoffrey W. Bromiley. Edinburgh: T & T Clark.

Rehberg, Karl-Siegbert. 1988. "Arnold Gehlen's Elementary Anthropology: An Introduction." Introduction to *Man: His Nature and Place in the World* by Arnold Gehlen, ix–xxxvi. New York: Columbia University Press.

Rothacker, Erich. 1934. "Geschichtsphilosophie." In *Handbuch der Philosophie: Staat und Geschichte*. Edited by A.Bäumler & M. Schröder. München & Berlin: Verlag R. Oldenbourg.

Scheler, Max. 1961. *Man's Place in Nature*. New York: The Noonday Press.

Schultz, Peter. 1999. "Selbsterhaltung als Paradigma der modernen Rationalität: Zur Legitimation neuzeitlicher Subjektivität." In *Die Kunst des Überlebens: Nachdenken über Hans Blumenberg*. Edited by Franz Josef Wetz & H. Timm, 244–265. Frankfurt am Main: Suhrkamp Verlag.

Sherrington, C.S. 1942. *Man on his Nature*. Cambridge: Cambridge University Press.

Spiegelberg, Herbert. 1972. *Phenomenology in Psychology and Psychiatry: A Historical Introduction*. Evanston: Northwestern University Press.

Stirk, Peter M. R. 1992. *Max Horkheimer: A New Interpretation*. Hemel Hempstead: Harvester Wheatsheaf.

Thies, Christian. 2007. *Arnold Gehlen zur Einführung*. Hamburg: Junius.

Wetz, Franz Josef. 2009. "The Phenomenological Anthropology of Hans Blumenberg." *Iris* 1(2): 389-414.

Anti-Federalism and the Question of Constituent Power in the American Constitutional Debate

Benjamin Popp-Madsen*

Constituent Power and the Neglected Opposition to the American Constitution

The concept of founding new political regimes has in the history of political thought mainly been understood as the workings of a mythical lawgiver or through the theoretical, hypothetical construct of the state of nature. But in the American context—as James Madison was well aware in Federalist no. 38 (Madison 1961, 227–236)—the constitution was written and ratified after popular discussions, town hall meetings, deliberations and conventions. The Anti-Federalists—the group of politicians and public figures who argued against the ratification of the constitution—were also conscious of the special way foundings, alterations and politics in general had been conducted in the new world; they also celebrated what Gordon Wood in *Creation of the American Republic* has labelled as politics conducted by the people-out-of-doors (Wood 1969, 319). DeWitt (1986, 189) notes that "from the first settlement of the country, the necessity of civil associations, founded upon equality, consent and proportionate justice have ever been universally acknowledged." As such, the American Revolution in 1776 and the adoption of the constitution in 1788 are good examples of Lockean social contract theory in practice, with the two successive steps of forming an original political community (codified in the Declaration of Independence) and instituting a form of government (codified in the American Constitution). This article will investigate the second contractual moment of American politics, and the paradoxical loss of the constituent power in the very moment of the ratification of the constitution. This will be done through a detailed analysis of the constitutional debate between the Federalists and the Anti-Federalists; a more loosely organized group composed by John DeWitt, Patrick Henry, Melancton Smith and the pseudonym writers Centinel, Brutus, Cato and the Federal Farmer.

* Benjamin Popp-Madsen is a ph.d student in political science at the University of Copenhagen.

The Anti-Federalists have played a peculiar and often neglected role in the debates on constituent power and the American Revolution. Even though Hannah Arendt in *On Revolution* discusses the lost treasure of the revolutionary spirit, and insightfully states that "it was the Constitution itself, this great achievement of the American people, which eventually cheated them of their proudest possession" (Arendt 1963, 231), she does not discuss the actual Anti-Federalist opposition to the constitution. Antonio Negri understands in a similar fashion the American Constitution to be decisive moment in the history of the constituent power; the moment of the tragic transformation of the concept and its complete appropriation by liberal constitutionalism: "By now, the constitutional motor is marching, even hastening forward. The masterpiece of transferring the constituent foundation from the people to the constitution is fully realized already at the end of the first part of The Federalist" (Negri 1999, 165). Again, the omission of the political actors who argued against this transformation of the constituent power is significant.[1]

In more general writings on the American Revolution the Anti-Federalists play an analogous role. Herbert Storing describes the Anti-Federalists as conservative, agrarian politicians afraid of changing the status quo (Storing 1981, 7–23), and Gordon Wood writes the Anti-Federalists off as "state-centered men with local interests and loyalties only, politicians without influence and connections, and ultimately politicians without social and intellectual confidence" (Wood 1969, 486), and thus the debate between the Federalists and the Anti-Federalists does not even qualify as political, but instead "the struggle over the constitution, as the debate of nothing else makes clear, can best be understood as a social one" (Wood 1969, 484).

As such, the Anti-Federalists—even though they were the principal critics of the centralization of power and the aristocratic elements in the constitution—are either neglected (Arendt, Negri) or ridiculed (Storing, Wood). One theoretical explanation of this peculiar treatment of the Anti-Federalists is the dominance and interrelatedness of concepts such as size, space and representation in writings on the American revolutionary period. For Negri, for example "the battles and the political alternatives taking place here assume the organization of space as their specific object" (Negri 1999, 142), and for Wood the transition from a confederation of small republics with direct representation to a federal state covering extensive territory and employing multiple representational mechanisms, is magnified into "the end of classical

---

1 For a contemporary omission of the Anti-Federalists, see Jean Cohen's work on federations (2011).

politics" (Wood 1969, 606), and the complete replacement of republicanism with liberalism. Although more nuanced and in opposition to Wood's depiction, Andreas Kalyvas and Ira Katznelson also understands the American debate through size and representation (and also omits the Anti-Federalists), as representation is precisely the Madisonian answer to the problem of size in the making of an extensive republic for the moderns (Kalyvas and Katznelson 2008, 88–117).

On the contrary, recent historical scholarship culminating in Saul Cornell's seminal *Anti-Federalism & the Dissenting Tradition in America, 1788–1828* (1999) has acknowledged the described tendency to omit or ridicule the Anti-Federalists (Cornell 1989, 39; Cornell 1999, 1). This recent historical engagement with the Anti-Federalists is—like the attempt of this article—"motivated by the desire to expose an alternative American political tradition and to uncover a political path not taken" (Cornell 1989, 39). In illuminating this untaken path, many historical commentators have depicted the Anti-Federalists positively and have associated their localism and distrust in centralization with a specific theory of democracy and representation (Cornell 1989, 46, 1999, 3; Howe 1989, 3; Rose 1989, 75; McWilliams 1989, 22–25). To these commentators, the Anti-Federalists were aware of the inherent dangers in what Alexander Hamilton called a consolidated government, i.e., a sovereign state; these dangers being the lack of local democracy and direct participation and the dismantling of a vibrant public sphere. As Sheldon Wolin has argued in his powerful essays on the bicentennial celebration of the American constitution in *The Presence of the Past: Essays on the State and the Constitution* (1989), by ratifying the constitution a specific way of understanding politics was chosen and another way was lost. This lost Anti-Federalist way of politics is for Wolin directly associated with "the loss of democratic hopes" (Wolin 1989, 4). In a similar way, Carol Rose has very convincingly shown how the debate between the Federalists and Anti-Federalists resembles the earlier European debate between Royalists and Anti-Royalists, and how the Federalists shared their royalist forerunners concern of the weakening of government by popular influence (Rose 1989, 85–92). I will return to this historical scholarship later in article.

In opposition to the described derision of the Anti-Federalists and the extensive focus on *size* in the debates on the American constitutional struggle, and form the constituent power, I propose to discuss and explore the Anti-Federalists not through the notion of representation and space, but through the notion of *time*. Obviously, the Anti-Federalists *did* discuss representation, space and size (DeWitt 1969, 329–335; "Cato" 1969, 336–341; "Brutus" 1969, 345–358), and even linked them together arguing against Madison's famous meditation on factions in Federalist no. 10: "We dissent, first, because it is the opinion of the most celebrated writers on government, and confirmed by uniform experience, that a very extensive territory cannot be governed on the principles of freedom, otherwise than by a confederation of republics" ("Centinel" 1969, 249). However, in a more general manner, if we take the perspective of the constituent power, the Anti-Federalists were occupied with a certain question of *time*: what is to be done after a revolution? How to keep the spirit that guided the revolution alive after the moment of foundation? How to make sure that the people during the temporal gap between the two Lockean contracts, do not forget the spirit of the first moment of foundation, and waste it in the second moment of the institution of government?

These questions, I think, are key in understanding the novelty and radicalism of the Anti-Federalists, and to reconfigure the American constitutional debate not as a debate between republicanism and liberalism (Wood), not as different modalities of the relationship between space, size and representation (Negri, Kalyvas, and Katznelson), and not as conservative agrarians *contra* progressive, capitalist metropolitans (Storing), but as a debate between two types of sovereignty: sovereignty as the supreme command of the state, and sovereignty as the constituent power of the people. This is similar to the way that both Wolin (1989, 82–88) and Cornell (1999, 303–309) have depicted the debate.

The questions, which the Anti-Federalists posed concerning the relationship between time, constituent power and the revolutionary aftermath, were certainly not new. Machiavelli had already in his remarkable notion of refoundation as augmentation in *The Discourses* described refoundation as the necessary return to the origins: "The way to renovate them [constitutions], as have been said, is to reduce them to their starting-points" (Machiavelli 1983, 385–386). He was thus aware of the negative influence on time to the revolutionary achievement. [2] Arendt grappled with the same question in her discussion on the conflict between the council system and the professional revolutionary parties, which over time had destroyed every revolution (Arendt 1963, 207–274). So did the Marquis de Condorcet in his development of his

---

2 So was Aristotle in *Politics*, book 5, where he developed an entire theory of the cyclical change of constitutions and regimes due to the inevitable corruption and decay of institutions, and Aristotle understood these changes directly as "political revolutions" (Aristotle 1954, 214).

model of primary assemblies with participation from below (Cordorcet 1976, 151–153). But the most famous formulation of the relationship between time, revolution and constituent power is that of Thomas Jefferson and Thomas Paine, and their shared idea of the power of living over the dead: "Can one generation bind another, and all others, in succession forever? I think not. The Creator has made the earth for the living, not for the dead" (Jefferson 1999, 386). Paine echoed him in *Rights of Man*: "The vanity and presumption of governing beyond the grave is the most ridiculous and insolent of all tyrannies" (Paine 1969, 138).

Already some years before Paine's statement and contemporary to Jefferson, however, the Anti-Federalists struggled to convince the American public of the dangers inherent in the proposed constitution. They tried to convince their opponents that the revolutionary spirit, which had founded the American confederation twelve years earlier, would be destroyed if the constitution were adopted.

In order to understand the theoretical consequences for the constituent power and its relation to foundations of new political regimes and subsequent institutionalization, I will trace the detailed, rich and contextual debate between the Federalists and the Anti-Federalists in 1787–1788, and seek to understand it as a debate between two types of sovereignty. It thus becomes an American update of the earlier debate on sovereignty, federalism and revolution in sixteenth and seventeenth century Europe. In order to show this, the article will be structured in the following way: a) an analysis of *The Federalist Papers* in order to show how the essential aspiration of the Federalists was the construction of Hobbesian or Bodinian sovereignty, b) an interpretation of the basic Anti-Federalist question as a question of time, that is, a question of how to preserve the revolutionary spirit, c) finally, a discussion of the Anti-Federalists answer to the problem of time, namely the discovery of the federal principle.

The American Leviathan: *The Federalist Papers*
From October 1787 to May 1788 Hamilton, Madison and Jay issued eighty-five newspaper articles arguing in favour of the ratification of the constitution, and the articles understanding of republicanism, constitutionalism and the division of powers have become dominant in American political theory. In this section, I propose to read *The Federalist Papers* as an argument for unified state sovereignty in the Bodinian and Hobbesian tradition. As such, it becomes one of history's most extensive deceptions that Hamilton, Madison

and Jay took the name *Federalists*, as they argued against the *real* Federalists, that is, the Anti-Federalists.

The central argument in *The Federalist Papers* is the that choice between the Constitution and the Articles of Confederation is in fact a choice between stability and anarchy, between security and violent struggle—in short a Hobbesian choice: "Among the many objects to which a wise and a free people find it necessary to direct their attention, that of providing for their safety seems to be the first" (Jay 1961, 36), and to obtain this first principle of politics a strong sovereign is required, otherwise the "division of the States into distinct confederacies of sovereignties" will equal "a number of unsocial, jealous, and alien sovereignties" (Jay 1961, 32–33). Ultimately, it is a choice between "an adoption of a new Constitution or a dismemberment of the Union" (Hamilton 1961, 31), or with Hobbes: anarchy or sovereignty. Whereas Jay's papers no. 2–5 are concerned with the advantages of the union in relation to external dangers from other nations, Hamilton's papers no. 6–9 are concerned with internal conflict and sedition. Just as nations are in a state of nature with each other, so would the confederate states be without a sovereign national government: "To look for continuation of harmony between a number of independent, unconnected sovereignties situated in the same neighbourhood would be to disregard the uniform course of human events, and to set at defiance the accumulated experience of ages" (Hamilton 1961, 48). Thus, the freedom the Americans obtained with the revolution, and which according to Arendt is the sole goal of every revolution (Arendt 1963, 19), must—in order for the Americans to become a real nation—give way for security or *raison d'état*: "Safety from external danger is the most powerful director of national conduct. Even the ardent love of liberty will, after a time give way to its dictates ... To be more safe, they at length become willing to run the risk of being less free" (Hamilton 1961, 61–62). Here we can see the Federalists understanding of the relation between constituent power and time: the revolution granted freedom, but in order not to fall back into "the pernicious labyrinths of European politics and war" (Hamilton 1961, 60), security needs to be provided at the very expense of freedom. This hierarchical relation is confirmed to an even greater extent when Madison in Federalist no. 49 discusses the idea of a recurrent appeal to the people in moments of crises: "there appear to be insuperable objections against the proposed recurrence to the people" Madison stated, and these being that "frequent appeals would, in great measure, deprive the government of that veneration which time bestows on everything, and without which perhaps the wisest and freest governments would not possess the required stability" (Madison 1961, 311). In short, *time* itself, in Madison's understanding, requires that the freedom of the founding ought to be replaced with the stability of government; stability in other words requires that a political community abstains from returning to its principal source of legitimacy, that is, to the constituent power of the people.[3] It is exactly this relationship between time, stability and freedom that the Anti-Federalists challenge, and which I will discuss in section three.

So far, the Federalists have posed the problem of unity in a completely Hobbesian vocabulary of the passionate and evil human nature, the inevitability of conflict, and the trade of freedom for the ultimate political value of security. Moreover, the federalist solution is also strictly Hobbesian: "Government implies the power of making laws. It is essential to the idea of a law that it be attended with a sanction; or, in other in words, a penalty or punishment for disobedience" (Hamilton 1961, 105), or as Hobbes himself famously stated in *Leviathan*: "covenants without the sword are but words, and of no strength to secure man at all" (Hobbes 1994, 106). In order to establish a secure republic, which is governable, the Federalists wanted to destroy all the intermediate layers of political community, corporations, pledges and promises that theorists of the constituent power from Marsilius of Padua (Marsilius 2005) over Johannes Althusius (Althusius 1995) and Condorcet to Arendt all relied on. Instead a direct, hierarchical relation between the sovereign and the subject is necessary in order to govern and establish safety: "we must extend the authority of the Union to the persons of the citizens—the only proper objects of government" (Hamilton 1961, 105). The Anti-Federalists must give up their "blind devotion to the political monster of an *imperium in imperio*" (Hamilton 1961, 103). According to the analysis of the historical similarity between the political aspirations of the Federalists and the earlier European royalists made by Carol Rose, this attempt to nullify all intermediate political layers between the state and the subjects has always been primary object of monarchist politics. As such, Rose understands the Federalists as a continuation of what was originally royalist political goals as "our own Revolution was in some ways just another in a long line of revolts of provincial privilege against centralizing royalist pretension" (Rose 1989, 81).

In short, instead of the corporatist theory of the constituent power and a political community held together by multiple pledges and contracts between

---

3 The question is not whether the people are the source of legitimacy "*as the people are the only legitimate fountain of power*" (Madison 1961, 310), but whether they should be appealed to in moments of crises and exception—that is, whether the constituent power should be re-activated.

numerous layers of power, the Federalists aspired for classical Bodinian sovereignty as the "absolute and perpetual[4] power of a commonwealth ... that is, the highest power of command" (Bodin 1992, 1).

No attempt to argue that the Federalists aspired for Bodinian or Hobbesian sovereignty would be complete without a discussion of Madison's famous paper no. 10. For Madison, the main political problem for a republic is the problem of factions; and the problem cannot be solved in the small, confederate republics due to the problem of majoritarianism (Madison 1961, 76). Instead, only through extending the size of the republic and channelling the opinions of the people through a series of complex representational mechanisms can the factional disaster be avoided. As Wilson McWilliams has argued, Madison and the Federalists employ here a very distinct understanding of representation. The representatives ought not to be familiar with their constituencies, and should not debate and deliberate with them. Only by distancing themselves from the electors could they reach the objective public interest: "the Federalist doctrine of representative government can be reduced to a single concise principle: Objective interests, objectively arrived at" (McWilliams 1989, 15).

With this "republican remedy for diseases most incident to republican government" (Madison 1961, 79), the Federalists reach the apex of their Hobbesianism: social life is nothing but factional strife, the end of politics is nothing but the control of these factional conflicts. The instrument to this end is the creation of a system where the people only exists through representation and cease to be existentially present so that the "society will be broken down into so many parts, interests and classes of citizens" (Madison 1961, 321). This picture of political reality is combined with the Hobbesian obsession with security over freedom, with the Hobbesian fear of the people as existentially present outside the constitution—manifest in Madison's warning against re-experiencing the foundational moment. This finally becomes combined with the Bodinian demand for a direct hierarchical relation between the sovereign and the subject.

Essentially, the Federalists wanted to refuse the Americans the same experience of freedom and founding that they experienced with the Declaration of Independence in 1776, and instead replace these expressions of freedom with

---

4 Again, we see the Federalists understanding of the relation between time and constituent power through a very interesting semantically similarity: Sovereignty has to be perpetual. Compared to Jefferson's idea that "no society can make a perpetual constitution, or even a perpetual law" (Jefferson 1999, 596), this is a radically different understanding of time.

perpetual sovereignty: "Stability, on the contrary, requires that the hands in which power is lodged should continue for a length of time the same. A frequent change of men will result from a frequent return of elections; and a frequent change of measures from a frequent change of men: whilst the energy in government requires not only a certain duration of power, but the execution of it by a single hand" (Madison 1961, 223). In short, even though Hamilton accused the Anti-Federalists of creating the political monster of *imperium in imperio*, it was the Federalists who created an American Leviathan.

The Anti-Federalist Question of Time: How to Keep the Revolutionary Spirit Alive?

"What if there is no other way?" Negri asks, "What if the very condition for maintaining and developing the juridical system were to eliminate constituent power?" (Negri 1999, 10). For the Federalists there indeed is no other way: the adoption of the constitution means the elimination of the constituent power. On the contrary, the Anti-Federalists' answer to the problem of time, and the hereby related conflict between constituent power and its constituted achievements is completely different, and delivered in two steps: a) an analysis of the constitution and the writings of the Federalists as precisely an attempt to eliminate the constituent power, that is, the identification of the problem of keeping the revolutionary spirit alive (elaborated in this section), b) a positive answer to this question through the discovery of the federal principle as the political form of freedom (elaborated in the next section).

As noted in the introduction, the Anti-Federalists do not represent a cohesive group, and their political arguments are not as clear and persuasive as Madison's and Hamilton's. Thus, in order for the radicalism of the Anti-Federalists to emerge, a theoretical reconstruction of their arguments is necessary.

What *did* unite the Anti-Federalists was their opposition to the constitution, and the shared awareness of the implicated loss of the constituent power. In the words of John DeWitt, with direct reference to the Bodinian definition of sovereignty, "it is not temporary, but in its nature, perpetual. It is not designed that you shall be annually called, either to revise, correct or renew it; but, that you shall grow up under, and be governed by it, as well as ourselves. It is not so capable of alterations as you would at first reading suppose; and I venture to assert, it can never be, unless by force of arms" (DeWitt 1986, 195). Here, DeWitt recognized that the ratification of the constitution would be a Hobbesian self-fulfilling prophecy: if the constitution does not allow for public alterations, then, ultimately, it will be a choice between sovereignty and anarchy, as the constitution can be altered only by *force of arms*, that is, by returning to the state of nature.

The same concern is expressed by the Anti-Federalist Patrick Henry: "we may fairly and justly conclude, that one-twentieth part of the American people, may prevent the removal of the most grievous inconveniences and oppression, by refusing to accede to amendments" (Henry 1986, 205). This concern strikes at the heart of problems of constituent power and time insofar as the constituent subject tendentiously loses its authority and becomes alienated by what it has constituted. In political terms, this is problem of tyranny and tyrannicide, which were the central issue for the French Monarchomacs, as well as Henry: "My great objection to this government is, that it does not leave us the means of defending our rights; or, of waging war against tyrants" (Henry 1986, 203). He furthermore argued that the adoption of the constitution would be yet another historical "instance of the people losing their liberty by their own carelessness and the ambition of the few" (Henry 1986, 202). Instead, Henry directly links constituent power and popular sovereignty together because "whenever any government shall be found inadequate, or contrary to these purposes, a majority of the community hath, and undubitable, unalienable and indefeasible right to reform, alter, or abolish it, in such manner as shall be judged most conducive to the public weal. This, Sir, is the language of democracy" (Henry 1986, 206).

These arguments can also be found in the pseudonym writer "Brutus," who expresses the same concerns as DeWitt and Henry: "the people in general would be acquainted with very few of their rulers; the people at large would know very little of their proceedings, and it would be extremely difficult to change them" ("Brutus" 1986, 292). This was because "many instances can be produced in which the people have voluntarily increased the powers of the rulers; but few, if any, in which rulers have willingly abridged their authority" ("Brutus" 1986, 283).

We can now begin to see the Anti-Federalists understanding of the relationship between constituent power, the constituted order and time: the achievement of the constituent power—the constitution—will over time alienate itself from its principle source of legitimacy—the people—and thus the split between legitimacy (the constituent power of the people) and legality (the constitution) will render every further appeal to the constituent power illegal. Due to this split between legitimacy and legality, the Anti-Federalists argue, constitutional changes can only happen illegally through violent struggles.

The Anti-Federalists in the very midst of the constitutional debate provide us with the same insight which Arendt presents nearly two hundred years later in *On Revolution*, namely that the ratification of the constitution is equal to the destruction of the revolutionary spirit: "When the American spirit was in its youth, the language of America was different: Liberty, Sir, was then the primary object ... But now, Sir, the American spirit, assisted by the ropes and chains of consolidation, is about to convert this country to a powerful and mighty empire" (Henry 1986, 209). [5] Two important elements are obvious from this quote: first, the Arendtian vocabulary of the lost spirit of the revolution as the spirit of freedom, and secondly, that this loss is due to a certain political form: the consolidated, sovereign state with imperial characteristics.

As such, the aim for the Anti-Federalists was not the depreciation of government in general. Nor was it the idea of a non-institutionalized, ever-present constituent power in permanent revolution, as Negri would have it (Negri 1999, 225). Rather, it was a critique of a *specific* way to institutionalise politics which made it difficult to change the basic constitutional norms of the community. To see how Anti-Federalists criticized the political form of state sovereignty and to understand why the emergence of constituent power stands in opposition to the state form, it is necessary to analyse the arguments which the Anti-Federalists provided in direct response to the two main arguments of the Federalists, namely the Hobbesian hierarchy of security over freedom, and the Bodinian aspiration for a direct relation between sovereign and subject.

As described in the section above, the Federalists imagined a more energetic government by destroying the intermediate layers of states, contracts and promises, and by establishing a direct relation between the sovereign and the subject. For the Anti-Federalists, this attempt was inscribed in the very first line of the proposed constitution: "America may depend on this: Have they said, we the States? Have they made a proposal of a compact between states? If they had, this would be a confederation: It is otherwise most clearly a consolidated government. The question turns, Sir, on that poor little thing—the expression, We, the people, instead of the States of America" (Henry 1986, 199). The same analysis is made in the Pennsylvania Minority Statement after the state's ratification of the constitution: "The preamble begins with the words, 'We the people of the United States,' which is the style of a compact between individuals entering into a state of society,

---

5 Consolidation is the word the Federalists used for sovereignty (Hamilton 1961, 30).

and not that of a confederation of states" ("Centinel" 1986, 254). Thus, the
Anti-Federalists clearly understood that the Federalists and the language of
the constitution performed exactly the same theoretical operation that Hobbes' did in *Leviathan*: social contract theory from medieval political theory
over Althusius and until Hobbes was always a contract between pre-existing
political communities, city states or provinces (Gierke 1913, 6–7). Thus Hobbes' radicalism lay in his appropriation of this tradition, and the subsequent
individualization of it. This is precisely the critique made by the Anti-Federalists. By changing the preamble from "We, the States" to "We, the People,"
the constitution envisions its own production as a result of pre-political individuals contracting in a state of nature rather than numerous pre-existing
political communities coming together, with the obvious consequence of
creating "a monarchy, like England—a compact between Prince and people"
(Henry 1986, 200).

Besides the critique of the replacement of a communal social contract with
a liberal individualist one, the Anti-Federalists furthermore engage critically
with the idea of security as the prime political value. The argument of the
Federalists had been Hobbesian in essence: in order to avoid external danger
and to forge internal unity, security must be prioritized over freedom. The
Anti-Federalists re-inverted this argument. For Henry "The first thing I have
at heart is American liberty; the second thing is American union" (Henry
1986, 215). The end of politics for the Anti-Federalists was thus not commercial prosperity or imperial ambition, but freedom: "You are not to inquire
how your trade may be increased, nor how you are to become a great and
powerful people, but how your liberties can be secured; for liberty ought to
the direct end of your government" (Henry 1986, 200). Importantly, the freedom the Anti-Federalists have in mind is not liberal, private freedom, but the
public, political freedom of self-government: "There can be no free government where the people are possessed of the power of making laws by which
they governed ... in their own persons" ("Brutus" 1986, 345).

As such, the Federalists and the Anti-Federalists had completely different
ontologies of the political: for the Federalists, the political emerges as a contract between individuals for the sake of security, the social world is dominated by factional conflict, and the sole aim of government is the reduction of
factional influence by dispersing popular interest as much as possible. On the
contrary, for the Anti-Federalists, the political is a product of an agreement
between already formed political communities in order to cooperate, and the
goal of government is the enhancement of public freedom.

In summary, the debate between the Federalists and the Anti-Federalists can be reinterpreted as a debate between two different types of sovereignty as Andreas Kalyvas' ideal typically has developed them (Kalyvas 2005): state sovereignty as a command in the Bodinian and Hobbesian tradition and sovereignty as the constituent power of the people.

It has become apparent from the comparison so far that the main difference between these two types of sovereignty is their altogether different configuration of the relationship between foundation (constituent power), constituted order and time: through an understanding of the foundation as a contract between individuals, a notion of social life as conflictual, and the appraisal of security as the highest political value, Federalists recommended the impossibility of returning to the foundations (Madison in papers no. 49–50) and advocated for the temporal exhaustion of the constituent power and the revolutionary spirit in the constituted order. The political form which could achieve these goals could only be the sovereign state. The Anti-Federalists configuration of the concepts is different. As political institutions can only be an agreement between already existing political communities in the endeavour for freedom, it is necessary that the constructed institutions have inherent mechanisms for refoundation as the temporal distance between the original new beginning and the present will always corrupt the spirit of the foundation.

The temporal corruption of political institutions has been a common theme in the history of political thought from the Aristotelian and Polybian understandings of inevitable cyclical change of regime forms, over Machiavelli's idea of refoundation as returning to the origins and Jefferson's and Paine's revolt of the living, up to the modern expression of Weberian institutional routinization. Thus, the divide between the Federalists and the Anti-Federalists exists in fact that the Federalists due to their political ontology welcomes this routinization as necessary, whereas the Anti-Federalists criticize it because of the loss of freedom and constituent power. Whereas the state form—Hamilton's energetic and consolidated government—becomes emblematic of the necessary routinization and lack of appeal to the founding moment, the extremely important and unresolved question is (I think this is the question with which the Anti-Federalists were occupied) which form of political organization, if any, accommodates the re-emergence of the constituent power. In other words: with the interpretation of the basic Anti-Federalist question as a question of how to keep the revolutionary spirit alive after the founding moment; it is now time to look at their solution.

The Anti-Federalists Answer: The Federal Principle

At first glance, the answer to the Anti-Federalist question is obvious: they are in favour of a federation, or what they called a confederation due to Hamilton's and Madison's strategic theft of the concept. As such, the Anti-Federalists argued in favour of a federation instead of a consolidated sovereign state. They were also well aware of the Federalists' aspirations: "Instead of being thirteen republics, under a federal head, it is clearly designed to make us one consolidated government" ('The Federal Farmer' 1986, 270) or as "Brutus" straightforwardly put it "all ideas of a confederation are given up and lost" ("Brutus" 1986, 284). The main argument against the constitution by the Anti-Federalists was, as described above, the future impossibility for the constituent power to reconfigurate the basic elements of the commonwealth. The important question is now to understand *why* the federal principle, *why* the federation as a political form, is better suited for revisiting the foundations than the state.

Just as the interpretation of the constitutional debate as conflict between the two types of sovereignty required a theoretical reconstruction of the arguments, so does an evaluation of the federal principle, as the Anti-Federalists were more eager to engage critically with the constitution than to lay out their own principles. When they did provide their own principles, as Cornell has argued, they were often more abstract and less potent than their federalist counterparts. This does not make the arguments weaker, but only more difficult to state cohesively and convincingly (Cornell 1999, 8).

For the Anti-Federalists, the federation was superior to the sovereign state form due to two characteristics: the internal freedom and participation in each republic and the external relations of equality, reciprocity, unanimity and cooperation between the states. As this political form was the Anti-Federalists' answer to the question of constituent power, constituted orders and time, and thus an attempt to go beyond the radical opposition and conflict between constituent power and constituted power in the sovereign state paradigm, I will discuss both characteristics starting with the internal advantages.

In the sovereign state, the infinite regress of legality will end in the factuality of the sovereign itself, as for example for Hans Kelsen and the legal positivism of his *groundnorm*, but in a federated republic with the ability to re-activate constituent power, both legality and legitimacy cannot come from above, only from below: "we at last arrive at some supreme, over whom there is no power to control but the people themselves. This supreme controlling power should be in the choice of the people, or else you establish an authority independent, and not amenable at all" ("Brutus" 1986, 354). Here, again, we see the intimate relationship between popular sovereignty and constituent power, as it is only if the people are sovereign, and not the consolidated government, that the institutions do not alienate themselves. Interestingly, the Anti-Federalists' institutional solution to how the people can remain sovereign has striking resemblances with other historical proponents of the constituent power: "In a pure democracy the people are the sovereign, and their will is declared by themselves; for this purpose they must all come together to deliberate, and decide. ... it must be confined to a single city, or at least limited to such bounds as that the people can conveniently assemble, be able to debate, understand the subject submitted to them, and declare their opinion concerning it" ("Brutus" 1986, 289). Firstly, in order for the constituent power to emerge, in order for the will of the people to be declared, the people must be existentially present, they must debate and decide in person. This notion of the people-as-presence is apparent in Rousseau's famous notion of the unrepresentable people (Rousseau 2002, 220), in Arendt's idea of public spaces as a necessity of politics (Arendt 1958, 50–58), and in Carl Schmitt's direct linkage between the people and the public, as there is "no people without public and no public without the people. By its presence, specifically, the people initiate the public" (Schmitt 2008, 272). The existential presence of the people is obviously impossible in the political set-up the Federalists imagined, both for reasons of size and space, but also for normative reasons as the people outside representation is nothing but violent factions. It is thus no coincidence that existing historical scholarship on anti-federalism stresses the crucial importance of their localism, not as a conservative introspective quality, but as an essential precondition for democratic self-rule (Cornell 1989, 59; 1999, 213–218; McWilliams 1989, 31; Rose 1989, 97).

Thus, again in accordance with the tradition of the constituent power, the political space has to be confined to a single city, as it is only this form of political organization, which allows for the presence of the people.[6] It is thus possible to understand the Anti-Federalists as the first thinkers of the ward system, which Jefferson describes in a very similar way as "Brutus" in his letters around 1815: "nearest to my heart, is the division of counties into wards. These will be pure and elementary republics, the sum of all which, taken together, com-

---

6 This conjunction of Rousseau, Arendt and Schmitt as thinkers of existential presence of the people obviously ignores the internal differences between the thinkers, namely their different understandings of how the people decide, when they are existentially present. Schmitt, inspired by Rousseau, sides with the will, whereas Arendt sides with deliberation.

poses the State, and will make the whole a true democracy" (Jefferson 1999, 219), and which Arendt appraised as the lost treasure of the revolution. Even Marx, when he discusses the Paris Commune in *The Civil War in France*, sides with communal ward system instead of the proletarian dictatorship and the seizing of the state as the first revolutionary step: "The Commune was formed of the municipal councillors, chosen by universal suffrage in various wards of the town, responsible and revocable at short terms" (Marx 1996, 184).[7] As such, it is only the single city ("Brutus"), the wards (Jefferson), the councils (Arendt) or the Communes (Marx), which makes the representatives *responsible and revocable at relatively short notice* (which is exactly what McWilliams shows in his comparison of the federalist and Anti-Federalist notions of representation [1989]), or translated into the language of the constituent power: it is only in these types of political communities that the constituent power can control its constituted institutions. In short, the federal principle for the Anti-Federalists (and Arendt, Jefferson and Marx) implies that internally in the elementary republics, the people have control over what they have instituted: "when a person authorises another to do a piece of business for him, he should retain the power to displace him, when he does not conduct according to his pleasure" ("Brutus" 1986, 356–357). As such, constituent power's control of its creations (that the representatives are responsible), and the continuing possibility for the constituent power to emerge (that the representatives are revocable), is the condition for freedom. Or, as the dissenters of ratification of the Virginia Convention phrased it in their proposed amendments: "all power is naturally invested in, and consequently derived from, the people; that magistrates therefore are their trustees and agents, at all time amenable to them … the doctrine of non-resistance against arbitrary power and oppression is absurd, slavish, and destructive to the good and happiness of mankind" (Amendment Convention 1986, 223).

Whereas all the Anti-Federalists observed the internal blessings of the federal form, the external advantages of a federation were less described and discussed. The most thorough account is given by the Anti-Federalist William Paterson, when he during the convention of the summer of 1787 proposed an opposition to the Virginia Plan; a plan which retained sovereignty

---

7 It is very interesting that Marx in his commentary on contemporary French politics in *The Eighteenth Brumaire of Bonaparte* (1852), and especially in *The Civil War in France* (1871), departs from what has come to known as the "mature" Marx: he understands revolution as a change in government, and not as the ultimate horizon and the end of politics, and he deliberately understands political institutions such as the Commune and political power to be important aspects of a revolutionary situation, and not as concepts withering away together with class distinctions.

in republics, had a "federal head"—as it was called—to coordinate cooperation among the states, and which became known as the New Jersey Plan. For
Paterson the fundamental principle of federal collaboration exists in "giving
each State a vote—and the thirteenth declaring that no alteration shall be
made without unanimous consent. This is the nature of all treaties. What is
unanimously done, must be unanimously undone" (Paterson 1986, 43). This
was that each state is "authorized to conclude nothing, but to be at liberty to
propose anything" (Paterson 1986, 45). Furthermore, there was to be "no
power to vary the idea of equal sovereignty," as the federal head receives its
legitimacy "immediately from the States, not from the people" (Paterson
1986, 43). Thus, the external relations between the states had to be grounded
upon plurality in agendas, but consent, equality and unanimity in decisions.
Furthermore, decisions are made directly by representatives from the federated states, who's mandate—as we saw above—is authorized directly by the
existentially present people.

In summary, the federation is the only political form the Anti-Federalists
imagined could keep the revolutionary spirit alive, precisely because it allows
for the constituent power to emerge both internally in the republics through
the ward system confined to single cities with more or less direct democratic
assemblies, but also externally as the states in cooperation through institutional principles such as freedom, equality, consent and unanimity can—following Patterson, *undo what has been done*; that is, they can politicise their own
foundations. Thus, the Anti-Federalists' countermove to the inevitable decay
of the revolutionary spirit and the routinization of constituted institutions is
a radical break with the state form and the command of the sovereign, and
the discovery of the federal principle.

Political Modernity and The Loss of the Constituent Power
The insights of this article are threefold: historical, analytical and normative.

Historically, the article argues against the omission of the Anti-Federalists
by Arendt and Negri and the derision by Storing and Wood. Following the
historical recovery of the Anti-Federalist especially made in the pioneering
work of Saul Cornell and the positive evaluation of their thinking, I break
with the understanding the of Anti-Federalists as local politicians occupied
with special interests, and I instead argue that the Anti-Federalists grappled with one of the most important questions in relation to the constituent

power: the question of time. The main problem for the Anti-Federalists—a problem raised in various ways by Machiavelli, Condorcet, Jefferson, Paine and Arendt—is how to keep the revolutionary spirit alive after the founding moment, and thus they argued for certain institutional mechanisms for the re-activation of constituent power. If we want to understand the radicalism of the Anti-Federalists, and not just see them as the losing part of a constitutional debate almost two hundred fifty years ago, I think it must be through the prism of the question of constituent power, foundational promises and institutional routinization over time.

Analytically, instead of understanding the American debate as a debate between republicanism and liberalism (Wood) or as different modes of relating size and representation (Negri), and instead of understanding the Federalists and the Anti-Federalists as aspiring to the same end but through different means, I suggest a radical opposition between them, and propose an interpretation of the debate as a conflict between sovereignty as command in the Bodinian and Hobbesian tradition and sovereignty as constituent power. This is as a debate between the state form and the federation. As such, the views of the Federalists and Anti-Federalists cannot be reconciled as they employ completely different political ontologies: security, individualism, hierarchical relations between sovereign and subject, and fear of both factions and of re-experiencing the foundational moment on the federalist side contra political freedom, corporatist and communal relations between multiple layers of power and an understanding of the necessity of refoundation and renewal on the Anti-Federalists side.

Finally, *normatively*, the paper has explored the reasons why the Anti-Federalists understood the federation as the political form of freedom and the form most suited for the re-activation of the constituent power. In short, for the Anti-Federalists, the revolutionary spirit can only be kept alive in a federation, not in a sovereign state. The reasons resemble those of Arendt and Schmitt in stressing the importance of the existential presence of the people in deliberation and decision. Furthermore, the institutional solution of confining the democratic assemblies to limited areas—a single city as "Brutus" put it—has striking similarities to Jefferson's ward system, Arendt's council system and Marx' appraisal of the Paris Commune.

In the end, in March 1789, the American Constitution came into effect, and the Anti-Federalists lost the constitutional debate. Thus, the founding moment, the revolutionary spirit and the constituent power was lost, as the constitution itself—the very creation of the constituent power—sealed off future possibilities of appeal to the principle source of democratic legitimacy in the people itself and replaced this possibility with the legality of the constitution and the command of the sovereign.

In this way, the American debate can be seen as an update of European debates on sovereignty, the state form and constituent power taking place in the sixteenth and seventeenth century between Jean Bodin, the Monarchomacs, Althusius and Hobbes, and which came to a historical conclusion with the construction of the European system of sovereign states with the treaty of Westphalia in 1648, and to a theoretical conclusion with Hobbes' *Leviathan* in 1651. It is thus the decisive experience of political modernity in both its European and American variants that a conflict between two types of sovereignty took place, that sovereignty as constituent power lost and was eradicated by sovereignty as command, and that the state form crushed all federal aspirations.

This meta-narrative points to exactly the same question of constituent power and time that the Anti-Federalists were occupied with. If political modernity is inaugurated by the new beginnings of the American and French revolutions, that is, by the emergence and achievements of the constituent power, and at the same time, if political modernity came to be characterized by the loss of the constituent power and the hegemony of the state form, then we must admit that the Anti-Federalists posed the necessary question for every radical politics, namely how to keep the revolutionary spirit alive after the foundation. How does one reconcile constituent power and constituted institutions without the latter exhausting the former? Whether the answer the Anti-Federalists have in common with Jefferson, Arendt and the communal Marx is right must be a question of coming political experimentation and democratic trial and error.

References

Althusius, Johannes. 1995. *Politica*. London: Liberty Fond Classics.

Arendt, Hannah. 1958. *The Human Condition*. Chicago: University of Chicago Press.

———. 1963. *On Revolution*. New York: Viking Press.

Aristotle. 1958. *The Politics of Aristotle*. Oxford: Oxford University Press.

Bodin, Jean. 1992. *On Sovereignty*. Cambridge: Cambridge University Press.

"Brutus." 1986. "Speeches." In *The Anti-Federalist Papers*, edited by Ralph Ketcham, 269–309, 324–336. New York: Signet Classics.

"Cato." 1986. "Speeches." In *The Anti-Federalist Papers*, edited by Ralph Ketcham, 317–324. New York: Signet Classics.

"Centinel." 1986. "Pennsylvania Minority Statement." In *The Anti-Federalist Papers*, edited by Ralph Ketcham, 237–256. New York: Signet Classics.

"Centinel." 1986. "Speeches." In *The Anti-Federalist Papers*, edited by Ralph Ketcham, 227–237. New York: Signet Classics.

Cohen, Jean. 2011. Federation. *Political Concepts 1*. Accessed January 27, 2014. http://www.politicalconcepts.org/issue1/federation/

Cornell, Saul. 1989. "The Changing Historical Fortunes of the Anti-Federalists." *Northwestern University Law Review* 84: 39–73.

Cornell, Saul. 1999. *Anti-Federalism & the Dissenting Tradition in America, 1788–1828*. Chapel Hill: The University of North Carolina Press.

de Condorcet, Marquis. 1976. *Selected Writings*. New York: Macmillan Publishing Company.

DeWitt, John. 1986. "Speeches." In *The Anti-Federalist Papers*, edited by Ralph Ketcham, 189–199, 311–317. New York: Signet Classics.

Gierke, Otto Von. 1913. *Political Theories of the Middle Age*. Cambridge: Cambridge University Press.

Henry, Patrick. 1986. "Speeches." In *The Anti-Federalist Papers*, edited by Ralph Ketcham, 199–217. New York: Signet Classics.

Howe, Daniel Walker. 1989. "Anti-Federalist/Federalist Dialogue and its Implications for Constitutional Understanding." *Northwestern University Law Review* 84: 1–11.

Hobbes, Thomas. 1994. *Leviathan*. Indianapolis: Hackett Publishing Company.

Jefferson, Thomas. 1999. *Political Writings*. Cambridge: Cambridge University Press.

Kalyvas, Andreas. 2005. "Popular Sovereignty, Democracy, and the Constituent Power." *Constellations* 12: 223–244.

Kalyvas, Andreas, and Ira Katznelson. 2008. *Liberal Beginnings: Making a Republic for the Moderns*. Cambridge: Cambridge University Press.

Machiavelli, Niccolo. 1970. *The Discourses*. London: Penguin Classics.

Madison, James, Alexander Hamilton, and John Jay. 1961. *The Federalist Papers*. New York: Signet Classics.

Marsilius of Padua. 2005. *The Defender of the Peace*. Cambridge: University of Cambridge Press.

Marx, Karl. 1996. *The Civil War in France*. In *Later Political Writings*. Cambridge: Cambridge University Press.

McWilliams, Wilson Carey. 1989. "The Anti-Federalists, Representation and Party." *Northwestern University Law Review* 84: 12–38.

Negri, Antonio. 1999. *Insurgencies: Constituent Power and the Modern State*. Minneapolis: University of Minnesota Press.

Paine, Thomas. 1969. *Essential Writings of Thomas Paine*. New York: Signet Classics.

Paterson, William. 1986. "Speeches." In *The Anti-Federalist Papers*, edited by Ralph Ketcham, 62–65. New York: Signet Classics.

Rose, Carol. 1989. "The Ancient Constitution vs. the Federalists Empire: Anti-Federalism from the Attack on "Monarchism" to Modern Localism." *Northwestern University Law Review* 84:74–105.

Rousseau, Jean-Jacques. 2002. *The Social Contract*. In *The Social Contract and the First and Second Discourse*. New York: Yale University Press.

Schmitt, Carl. 2008. *Constitutional Theory*. Durham: Duke University Press.

Storing, Herbert. 1981. *What the Anti-Federalists Were For*. Chicago: University of Chicago Press.

"The Federal Farmer." 1986. "Speeches." In *The Anti-Federalist Papers*, edited by Ralph Ketcham, 256–269 New York: Signet Classics.

Virginia Convention. 1986. "Proposed Amendments 27th June 1788." In *The Anti-Federalist Papers*, edited by Ralph Ketcham, 35–39. New York: Signet Classics.

Wolin, Sheldon. 1989. *The Presence of the Past: Essays on the State and the Constitution*. Baltimore: The John Hopkins University Press.

Wood, Gordon. 1969. *The Creation of the American Republic 1776–1787*. Chapel Hill: University of North Carolina Press.

Wasting a Day Chasing a Hare: Indolence, Self-interest and Spatial Mobility in the Rhetoric about Swedish Peasantry, ca. 1750–1850

Leif Runefelt*

Abstract

This article addresses the meaning of the concept of "indolence" (in Swedish, *lättja*) as it was used in various texts concerning the peasantry written by the Swedish social elite. The conclusion is that at exactly the point when the elite lost their ability to control and tax, they invoked the rhetoric of indolence. The spatial dimension was crucial, both where in relation to a peasant's home an activity took place, and how much effort it involved. I first use eighteenth-century literature touching the subject of peasant behaviours to illuminate the relationship between diligence and benefit, indolence and selfishness. I then turn to examples from a similar material from the early nineteenth-century, place descriptions, to take a close look at the relationship between spatially determined indolence and spatial mobility. Finally, both sets of source material are used in a discussion of what the ruling classes meant when they talked of indolence, and whether their rhetoric exposes a conflict over resources at the geographical peripheries of Swedish society.[1] My inspiration in this has been James C. Scott's (1998) thinking on the state and its relations with multifaceted, illegible local communities.

Of course, indolence, or rather the dichotomy of indolence and diligence, is held common across many contexts in early modern Europe. There is for instance an ethical and religious discourse on the idleness of the individual, as well as an ongoing discussion about the idleness of youth. In this article, the focus is strictly upon rural indolence as discussed in different types of Swedish literature on rural and agricultural issues. Methodologically, the article is a loose effort at a conceptual history demonstrating how the meaning of a continuously existing

---

* Leif Runefelt is associate professor of intellectual history in the Department of History and Contemporary Studies at Södertörn University.

---

1 By rhetoric, I mean not the rules of classic rhetoric, but rather the action-oriented statements that purpose to present as a true a specific account of a relationship that excludes alternative accounts.

concept, apparently uncomplicated and timeless, is in fact specific in terms of text and context. In the texts studied, indolence did not mean voluntary idleness or an unwillingness to work. Instead, the concept must be understood in relation to the concept of diligence, which in its turn was strongly connected to one specific activity—farming. Work, which was not farming, no matter how hard or fruitful, tended towards being conceived as indolence. Since farming is also spatially fixed, indolence was semantically connected to spatial movement.[2]

Rural Indolence—Some Introductory Examples

In a well-received essay, *Anmärkningar Om Södra Halland* (Notes on Southern Halland), published in the proceedings of the Royal Swedish Academy of Sciences in 1761, Johan Fischerström complained of the idleness of the county's inhabitants, bemoaning "that so many sections of society should be left to live in unproductiveness." Fischerström (1761a, 237, 276) gives reclaimed wetlands as an example, which "these Hallanders regarded as a punishment for their sins, and not at all the future farmland that', according to Fischerström, 'it actually was" (Fischerström 1761a, 237, quotation 276).[3] Southern Halland, far from being fertile agricultural land, was heavily wooded, with poor soil that was hard to work. Fischerström was not alone at the time in exclaiming over the general indolence of the people of Sweden's marshes, moors, and forests. In a doctoral thesis examined by Anders Berch only the previous year, *Tankar om Upodlings Möjelighet i Lappmarkerna* (On the Possibilities for Cultivation in Lapland) (1760), it was stressed that the potential for land reclamation and clearance was very high, but that peasants were not particularly interested. They were too busy hunting and fishing, activities that for Berch were not a sign of a lack of resources, but rather of indolence: the peasants were lazy and not much given to farming or land reclamation, while fishing and hunting were characterized as "pleasure and amusement" (Berch and Fjellström 1760, § 11).

Moving forward in time to the 1780s, the words of the widely travelled Abraham Hülphers can also serve as a useful example. In the last section of his exhaustive work on Lapland, *Samlingar til en Beskrifning* öfwer *Norrland* (Collections On a Description of Norrland), first published posthumously in 1922, he writes in a very similar vein to Anders Berch about the settlers there. His

---

2 I am inspired by the German tradition of conceptual history and its study of semantic fields; see Koselleck (1972, XXIf); Richter (1995, 48–50).

3 A similar notion of the inhabitants of Halland is found in Barchaeus' description of the county from 1773; Barchaeus (1924, 61).

point, however, was that it was local crafts that were neglected in favour of hunting and fishing:

> Handicrafts are practised very little by the settlers, who spend most of their time in fishing and hunting; the children, lacking occupation in their youth, become accustomed to indolence ["lättja"], and do very little before they are old enough to start fishing and going out into the woods. (Hülphers 1922, 161)

Still later, in 1824, the Lapland settlers were once again described in the same terms, this time by the later famous Evangelist preacher Lars Levi Læstadius. In his *Om möjligheten och fördelen af allmänna uppodlingar i Lappmarken* (On the Possibilities and Advantages of General Cultivation in Lapland), Læstadius announced that the Norrland peasants' fishing and hunting were evidence of their indolence and sloth; that they regarded it as too much effort to dig ditches, clear the land, and plough it: and that they were more inclined to go hunting and then lie about at home, idling: "But not the industrious man, who works by the sweat of his brow. Indefatigable work triumphs over all."[4]

One last example comes from the county of Medelpad in 1856, and the surveyor Olof Emanuel Næslund's description of the rural economy of the parish of Njurunda. He stressed how the district's forest industry had lured the peasants, and especially their sons and farmhands, away from the land, so that those who previously would have farmed now worked in forestry over the summer, earning enough to live an idle life of lethargic torpor during the winter. Næslund also brought up the subject of the herring fisheries, which posed a further threat, for a large part of the parish's population spent the winter making and mending nets, and then spent the summer out fishing. "Were all this work to be spent on cultivation, ditching, collection of manure, etc., then the people would be richly rewarded by the grateful soil" (Næslund 1945, 39–40, 60–61).

Breaking new ground in the Halland fens or the wide-open peatlands of the Norrland moors using nothing but fire, mattock, and shovel was an enormous task. It is perhaps not so surprising that an educated elite, caught up in

---

4 Læstadius (1981, 69). See also Runefelt (2008, 30, 37) for similar arguments used during Sweden's Age of Liberty. Note that not only does the penultimate sentence paraphrase the bible (Genesis 3:19), but the final sentence, "Oförtrutet arbete övervinner allt" (Work conquers all) is from Virgil's *Georgics*, 1: 145–146 (although the original—"*Labor omnia vicit improbus*"—is in the perfect tense, where, like the Christian Creation myth, it describes how Jupiter, following Saturn's Gold of Age, forced mankind to work hard for a living).

the fashionable enthusiasm for boosting national production, regarded the peasants as lazy.[5] The peasants' unwillingness to play along was an obstacle in Sweden's path to both greater prosperity and the lessening of its dependence on other countries. However, might there have been more to the characterization of the peasants as indolent than first meets the eye?

Eighteenth-Century Economic Literature: Indolence, Self-interest, and Community

Were Sweden's peasants truly lazy? Berch gave examples that to a degree contradicted his argument. He showed that the peasants in fact were industrious. They did not just laze about; they were busy fishing and hunting. Like his educated and powerful contemporaries, Berch had nothing against fishing and hunting per se. By way of contrast, another thesis, *Jämtelands djur-fänge* (The Hunt in Jämtland) (1753) commended hunting as a livelihood in a barely productive landscape, and fishing too was highlighted from time to time—for example, by the Royal Academy of Sciences—and promoted as useful to the nation.[6] However, diligence for its own sake is not interesting; it is the fruits of those labours, and to what use they are put, which are important. Diligence cannot be separated from benefit. That being the case, what then is idleness? Not doing anything, or not anything *useful*?

The early modern conception of indolence, just as with its antonym diligence, must be understood in the light of early modern ethics. The lazy choose to waste their time. The problem was not that they did nothing at all, but that they spent their time on things that were neither beneficial nor useful. Indolence is strongly connected with human self-interest and selfish desires. People long for an easy life, or at least what might be thought easiest in the circumstances. This longing means that they willingly lock themselves into various greed-induced behaviours: consumption, voluptuousness, sloth. All the things that make one feel good—for the moment. However, all these desires only concern people as individuals—their *own* needs, their *personal* benefit—and then only in the short term. Desire has no power to look to the future, or to look to the needs of others.

In social terms, those others can be "the greater good" or "the good of the community," meaning a regard for the needs of the wider community. Con-

---

5 Discussed in Runefelt (2008), again using the examples of Berch, Læstadius, and Fischerström.

6 Fishing, for example, by Nils Gisler in *Vetenskapsakademiens Handlingar*, 1748, 1751, and 1753, the first of which concludes with a call from the Academy for more reports on Swedish fishing; by Carl Fredrik Lund in *Handlingar* 1761; S[chultze] (1778)—see below.

sider one particular passage in Anders Berch's textbook on the new science of domestic economy, *Inledning til almänna hushålningen* (An Introduction to General Household Management) (1747) which illustrated his certainty as to the settlers' indolence and laziness. He starts by invoking natural law: people had come together and formed communities for mutual assistance and to avoid the chaotic license that characterized the natural state. In such civil societies, people waived some of their freedoms in order that they might enjoy the fruits of their shared labours. This work, however, was based on a clear division of duties, and on each and everyone understanding that they had a part to play in the whole. At heart, continued Berch, all the members of the community relied upon agriculture. This social division of labour, with its basis in agriculture, meant that the farmer had a duty, not only to work the land, but also to bring all available land into cultivation.

> In consequence whereof it is against all good management to leave any part of the land untilled, when its state is such that it might be reclaimed, or when no greater reason may be found as to why it should remain uncultivated. (Berch 1747, 161)

Clearly, for Berch and others considering the fate of rural Sweden, indolence was seen as a crime against the social division of labour. Fischerström too derives his views on society from natural law, and combines diligence, public benefit, and mutual interdependence in his chosen division of labour. What, then, were the duties of the peasant? Fischerström put great weight on the importance of agriculture and its much-neglected state in Sweden. Responsibility for this negligence could be laid at many people's doors: the educated and powerful (for which read the "Hat" faction in national politics), who chose to encourage factories and manufacturing instead of investment in agriculture; the major landowners, who because of their own cynical self-interest had fallen victim to the ungodly fallacy that peasants should be poor and ignorant.[7] The peasants themselves also bore some responsibility: they had neglected their farms for trade and other sidelines. Fischerström exclaimed:

---

7 The natural law argument is clear in Fischerström (1769, 7); responsibility for agriculture in Fischerström (1761b, 27–31, 48–49).

Orderliness in life is all, diligence is all, and, like the soul, is all. Without orderliness in the division of labour, good management cannot rise to its proper stature; without orderliness no society can achieve true wellbeing. (Fischerström 1761b, 71)

This orderliness was the division of labour in civil society, the agreed mutual dependency of all the members of the community. For the peasantry, this meant that they should always concentrate on farming the land.

It would be possible here to present a series of examples of how diligence was coupled to a division of labour justified by natural law, but space is limited, so a few must suffice. Fischerström's understanding was close to Johan Fredrik Kryger's, who discussed diligence and the division of labour in relation to concerns about national population shortages so typical of the period. Kryger thought indolence and commerce were greater problems in sparsely populated rural districts than elsewhere, because the large distances involved made the division of labour harder to sustain, and forced people to become more independent of one another. The peasant could not only be, as he should be, a peasant; he had to be a Jack-Of-All-Trades (Kryger 1758, 26).[8]

We find a similar formulation in the Swedish translation by Carl Fredrik Scheffer of a small part of the Marquis de Mirabeau's famous physiocratic work, *L'ami des hommes, Tankar om Sedernas Werkan På Folk-Mängden I et Land* (Notes on the Influence of Custom on the Population of a Country) (1759). It is well known that Fischerström was influenced by the physiocrats, and here we find ourselves once again in the company of the Hallanders. This was how things were meant to be:

Sand, moors, fens, all are serviceable and all can be rendered fruitful by labour. *Labor omnia vincit improbus.* Barrenness is never to be found, less through the fault of man. ... Industriousness draws out from the very bedrock the nectar needed for the best crops. ([Mirabeau] 1759, 12–13)[9]

Diligence was here strongly connected with the public good, and indolence became its opposite—all that which did not advance the common good. It was not just a question of idleness, of doing nothing, of being reluctant to work; it was all the activities that were not grounded in the maintenance of

---

8 The connection between the shortage of people, poor division of labour, and lack of industriousness was made by Westerman (1768, 11–12).

9 For the quotation from Virgil's *Georgics*, see above, n. 5.

the community's division of labour, and did not contribute to it. Two pairs of conceptual dichotomies thus stand out:

Indolence	Diligence
Selfishness	Public benefit

Just as Læstadius would maintain much later, there was felt to be a special relationship between diligence and working the land. Carl Carleson used the same biblical passage—Genesis 3:19—in the introduction to his *Tal Om span-måls-bristens afhjelpande* (On the Relief of the Grain Shortage) (1759): "One knows that the accursed earth properly speaking has no value; all her worth comes from the sweat of one's brow" (Carlsson 1759, 4). Diligence, duty, and benefit were all strongly connected to agriculture.

Berch's examination of the thesis *Jämtelands djur-fänge* (1749) is evidence of the fact that fishing and hunting were not necessarily seen as selfish; on the contrary, one passage showed that he saw the Lappland settlers' hunting as selfishness, while the type that Berch and the respondent Aeschill Nordholm wished to promote in the county of Jämtland would surely prove beneficial, once tried. Three pages of the thesis are devoted to the hare. Many people were said not to understand the usefulness of hare pelts, despite being excellent as, say, counterpanes: "Who does not know how good and warm hare-skin pelts are as bed-clothes?" If more people were to use hare-skin, large quantities of wool and sheepskin could be saved for other purposes (Berch and Nordholm 1953, 41–43, quote at 43). This sort of hunting—then unknown in Jämtland—was the *right* sort and thus counted as diligence. Meanwhile, the settlers' hunting was thought indolent because, far from being conducted for the public good, it was to its detriment. The actual work put in, whether measured in hours or labour, was entirely irrelevant.

The fact there was some debate as to whether those who went fishing and hunting were doing their bit for the community is perhaps the reason why the introductory chapter in Samuel Thomasson Schultze's *Den swenske fiskaren* (The Swedish Fisherman) (1778) drew a distinction between appropriate and inappropriate fishing.

The latter is the case when the peasant goes fishing when he should be ploughing; and the former when he attends to his small feats of fishing on the lake only when no task on the land has been neglected. (S[chultze] 1778, 7)

The proper task of the peasantry was thus to work the land. However, if they could supplement their larders by fishing, it was fine for them to do so: "thus tending the land is his first consideration, and the water a mere adjunct between times." Fishing tackle and techniques thus had to be chosen with care to ensure that no time was lost from farming.

Early Nineteenth-Century Place Descriptions: Indolence, Selfishness, and Spatial Mobility

In the writings of Berch, Fischerström, and Shultze the emphasis on agriculture had a spatial aspect. Hunting and fishing were mobile activities that took place away from the home, while farming was a stationary activity that to a large degree occurred close to home. While not totally evident in eighteenth-century sources, it became clearer in literature regarding agriculture and peasants of the nineteenth century. New concepts of scientific, or "improved," forms of cultivation, together with better profits in farming due to rises of grain prices, induced a substantial increase in this literature from the 1790s onwards. In this article, I confine myself to a representative genre within this literature: place descriptions from the period 1790–1860. A place description was a description of a specific, well-defined, agrarian local community—normally a parish of a hundred. Exactly what was described could vary, but the emphasis was on topics such as history and prehistory, topographic description, local customs, agriculture and the local economy, and the homes of local notables. It is plain that it was the agrarian elite who were responsible for the production of such place descriptions, and it is their point of view that is expressed, and not necessarily that of the authorities or the State (a common denominator for all literature on farming and peasants from the eighteenth and early nineteenth century is of course that nowhere were the voices of the peasants themselves to be heard). The descriptions can serve as examples of the ways in which members of the elite talked about the peasantry in terms of indolence. There are over seven hundred place descriptions of various sorts, and while elsewhere I have considered the genre in some detail, here I use some illustrative examples, with no claim to be comprehensive (Runefelt 2011; see also Adolfsson 2000, 34–35, and ch. 2).

The close family resemblance between the eighteenth-century literature on peasants and the nineteenth-century place descriptions can in fact be quite clear. When Major Elias Sandman described the parish of Lockne in Jämtland, which he said was typical of the county as a whole, for example, he condemned the peasantry for drifting into dilettantism and indolence while at the same time neglecting the land. Like Berch, he contrasted hunting and farming:

> Not unlike the hunter or fowler who wastes a day in chasing one hare, or one hazel hen, when with spade in hand he could have prepared a parcel of land, whereby he would have benefited his whole life long. (Sandman 1941, 61)[10]

To an even greater degree than the eighteenth-century literature on rural Sweden, the place descriptions had a markedly agrarian focus: agriculture was the staple industry, and all other forms of industry were always in its shadow. The place descriptions single out several problematic sidelines and a few advantageous ones. The fact that there were useful sidelines was self-evident, and it was recognized that agriculture alone was not enough to occupy peasant households, as it required very little activity for much of the year, due to the severity of the Swedish winter.[11] The authors of the place descriptions were well aware that many of Sweden's peasants were not able to live by farming alone, even when they owned their own land.

It is interesting here that many of the sidelines that were thought useful were associated with low spatial mobility. Three common examples were handicrafts, the manufacture of saltpetre, and linen production. The place descriptions' positive view of handicrafts was much of a part with political patronage in the widest sense, as Gustaf Utterström has observed, and found its clearest expression in the 1774 report of the Committee for Rural Husbandry set up by King Gustav III. It was thought that handicrafts could be pursued without curtailing agriculture, especially during the winter and in forest districts. Thus, handicrafts were regarded as promoting diligence, given that the peasantry had less to do in winter (Utterström 1957, ii. 23–26). The production of saltpetre was a very different matter. As an essential ingredient in gunpowder, its manufacture was in the national interest. It was thus essential that peasant communities contribute towards its production. The production of saltpetre was regulated and directed by the so-called Saltpetre Ordinances of the early nineteenth century. In the place descriptions there are pleas for an increase in saltpetre production, while at the same time it

---

10 The text was probably written in 1818.

11 Occasionally authors make much of the long winter nights as an opportunity for the populace to increase their wealth by greater industriousness. See, for example, Sefström (1984); Edelstam (1816, 36–37); Hesselgren (1823, 143).

was plain that a large proportion of Sweden's peasants chose to pay a cash saltpetre tax rather than actually deliver any saltpetre.[12] The place descriptions depict saltpetre production as entirely problem-free, with no negative consequences for farming, but in reality it demanded a substantial amount of manure, and could therefore cause problems for the peasants in an agricultural system whose chief problem was a shortage of fertilizer (Hesselgren 1823, 142–143).[13]

Linen production, in turn, was presented as especially useful, with the linen industry in the northern province of Hälsingland in particular held up as a model for the rest of the country. The place descriptions fell in with the line taken by the agricultural literature of the day, calling for more flax-growing and flax-dressing (Stiernström 1959, 39–40).[14] Linen production benefited the community in several ways. Firstly, linen was a primary article of consumption in Sweden that it was felt should not be imported; its production was therefore a patriotic duty. Secondly, flax-processing could take place during the winter when the peasantry had little else to do. Of course, linen production was only a sideline in a particular sense; it was also an occupation *within* agriculture, rather than alongside it, and it was not obvious that it should be thought to interfere with the peasants' primary activity. All peasants needed linen, and domestic production could therefore be seen as prudent thrift. Because flax-growing requires a fair amount of space it was mostly an option for areas with a great deal of newly cleared land, which in Sweden meant the northern regions, and the spread of flax in the early nineteenth century duly followed in the wake of land clearance. At the same time, linen met with ever-greater competition from imported cotton, which caused the industry considerable difficulties.[15]

Place descriptions such as Major Sandman's also addressed the detrimental sidelines. One example was given earlier: the peasants of Njurunda, who according to Næslund neglected their farms all year round in order to take part in the herring fishery. The problem appears to have been greatest in

---

12 Lamér (1815, 47); Edelstam (1816, 36–37); Sefström (1984, 25); Bernhard (1818, 42); Odencrants (1818, 59); Lagergren (1822, 177); Hielmquist (1823, 170); Wibelius (1849, 12).

13 For saltpetre production competing with agriculture, see Rask (1991, especially 285).

14 Another place description from Hälsingland that draws attention to flax cultivation is Ström (1964); see Lundell (2005, 73–74). Passing remarks or full advocacy of flax cultivation are very common in place description (see, for example, Lamér (1815, 43–44); Lindskog (1985, 374); Nordin (1827, 154).

15 For the broader advocacy of an increased cultivation of flax in Sweden, see Jonsson (1994, 15–16, 19–20, 26–7); and Utterström 1957, (ii. 64–5, 125–9).

coastal and border districts, and in the vicinity of towns. Fredric Wilhelm
Radloff asserted in his description of Roslagen (1804–5), the coastal area
northeast of Stockholm, that the archipelago's peasants harboured a dislike
of agriculture. Öhrströmer (1801) wrote of Väddö, an island in the same
archipelago, that the peasants there used their boats for freight while their
fields were overgrown with thistles, leaving them unable to support their families for much of the year (Radloff 1983, 380; Öhrströmer 1962, 15). Bexell
reported from the parish of Släp in Halland that farming there would provide significantly greater returns, if it were not for the fact that the heads of
the families and their sons concentrated on shipping, leaving the farming to
the farmhands. According to Johan Fredrik Hellberg (1824), the inhabitants
of Orust, a large island on the west coast, had for many years been led astray
by the large and easy profits to be had by neglecting their farms in favour of
herring fishing. In the event the problem solved itself when the herring runs
failed after 1808, although even as late as the mid-1850s many observers of
the coastal districts of Blekinge in south-east Sweden were of the opinion that
the peasantry were losing their appetite for agriculture because they spent
too much time at sea in their formative years (Bexell 1817–1819, iii. 406; Hellberg 1824, 10); Sylvén (1959, 4–6).

Claes Justelius (1813) thought that the inhabitants of Täby, outside Stockholm, neglected their farms because the close proximity of the capital offered
other ways to make a living. Bexell said the same thing of the peasants of
Abild, not far from Gothenburg. Among the later place descriptions, Adolf
Helander described Gothenburg's deleterious effect on the peasants of
Frölunda, who travelled to the city to sell goods at a profit, but once there it
was easy come, easy go as they frittered away their money—the peasantry's
extravagance and eagerness to shop in Gothenburg left them penniless and
heavily in debt (Justelius 1957, 10; Bexell 1817–1819, ii. 213; Helander 2001,
11, 19). The most damaging sideline otherwise was commerce, it too partly
a problem of geographical proximity. A great deal of time was spent trans-
porting goods, and many of the household's products were sold far afield. In
return, people bought what to the authors of the descriptions were unneces-
sary luxuries and general rubbish.[16]

With the place descriptions presenting these various sidelines in the dichot-
omous terms noted earlier, some were clearly thought to be the damaging
result of selfish behaviour, while others were beneficial to the public good.

---

16 For place descriptions' views on trade, see Runefelt (2011, 184–189).

The sidelines to be discouraged included Næslund's herring fishing, and herring fisheries in general. Excessive hunting and fishing were also included, as were trade and commerce—each characterized by spatial mobility and very much one with the discourse of idleness, indolence and neglect (anything but work). Finally, these sidelines were presented as being active choices on the part of those who thus decided not to work for the common good. The fact that a peasant fisherman's fields were overgrown with thistles was the choice, and fault, of the peasant. There was no attempt to explain the peasantry's behaviour in terms of risk-spreading, poor farming conditions, lack of resources, and the like. Instead, everything was reduced to a moral choice.[17] Thus, while the word "indolence" was seldom used, the concept was at work very actively within the place descriptions, as they showed how the peasants chose comfort and easy short-term profits instead of industrious toil on the fields.

The beneficial activities numbered agriculture and such sidelines as the production of saltpetre, linen cultivation, and rural handicrafts, all of which contributed to the public good. All these activities were localized, spatially speaking, with nitre made in special saltpetre houses, and flax grown in open fields and processed in the home. In the rhetorical sense, these sidelines were coupled with industriousness and diligence—a diligence that ensured that the household could satisfy its own needs by hard work.[18]

One striking example of how this was done was the contrasting of female diligence and male indolence. It was often the women of the household who spun and wove, and it was therefore no coincidence that it was exactly this form of female industriousness that gained praise.[19] The linking of indolence, selfishness and spatial mobility in the place descriptions left their authors peddling a moral caricature of the peasantry's gendered division of labour. Rosemarie Fiebranz, and Inger Jonsson before her, show that among the Hälsingland linen producers, the men took care of commercial transactions while the women handled the series of tasks needed in flax-processing: scutching, spinning, and weaving the linen (Fiebranz 2002, 110–111; Jonsson

---

17 For indolence, see, for example, Wahlenberg (1804, 26); Aspelin (1810, 18); Hesselgren (1823, 123); Hellberg (1824, 16); Sylvén (1929, 5–6); for the question of moral choice, see Runefelt (2011, 195f, 234–236).

18 For the connection to handicrafts, see Runefelt (2011, 152–7); for the connection to industriousness, see, for example, Bexell (1817–1819, ii. 35); Kilhman (1828, 50–51); Montelin (2007, 65); see also Utterström (1957, ii. 24); Jonsson (1994, 145).

19 For example, Radloff (1983, 380); Aspelin (1810, 21); Lagergren (1822, 178); Hesselgren (1823, 123); Nordin (1827, 146); Wibelius (1949, 8).

1994, 34–35, 204). In Carl Petter Ström's description of the parish of Färila (1827), in the heart of the region, women who stuck to their work in the home were commended as examples to follow, while the men were said to bring ruin on their households by travelling on business. The senior army surgeon Jonas Gestrich and the parish priest Christian Schönbeck also made the same point about the peasants of Jämtland and of Riseberga in the county of Skåne: nothing but ill came of the men's travelling on business, while the women's industriousness in the home was admirable (Ström 1964, 16–17; Fischerström 1761a, ii. 274–275; Gestrich 1817, 156; Schönbeck 1818, 31). Long before, in his description of the rural economy of southern Halland in 1761, Johan Fischerström had likewise commented on the fact that men were busy in commerce, deleteriousness though it was, and the women in praiseworthy weaving, spinning, and knitting of stockings, especially in the winter evenings. The conceptual dichotomies noted above can thus be complemented by a further pair:

Indolence	Diligence
Selfishness	Public benefit
Highly mobile	Fixed
Outside the home	In the home or close to home

The fact that the stockings and other products had to be got to market in order to be sold seems to have been thought irrelevant. The authors chose to present the peasantry's gendered division of labour in moral terms, with mobility an important negative factor.[20]

Legibility: The Elite's Filtered Vision

One fruitful approach to explaining the rhetoric about indolence, mobility, and selfishness is offered by James C. Scott's (1998) *Seeing Like a State: How Certain Schemes to Improve the Human Condition Have Failed*. Although Scott mostly concerns himself with authoritarian states in the twentieth century, he takes as his starting-point the breakthrough of science-based agriculture and forestry in late eighteenth- and early nineteenth-century Europe. Central to his argument is the concept of legibility. The nascent early modern state's need to tap its citizens' resources effectively by taxation was strongly hindered by the opaque nature of society, and as early as the seventeenth century, politicians

---

20 For the division of labour among the general populace when it came to flax processing, see Jonsson (1994, 29–36); and Fiebranz (2002, 110–111).

and thinkers began casting about for ways to increase clarity. Scott focuses on Colbert's policies in France, but he could equally well have discussed Axel Oxenstierna's fiscal policies or, perhaps even more fittingly, the late seventeenth- and early eighteenth-century attempts in political arithmetic to quantify everything within a country's borders using predetermined measures.[21]

According to Scott, this effort was directed more towards increased control than at taxation within the existing system. The eighteenth century, however, saw a broadening ambition for increased productivity—in other words, for a widening of the tax base— and the effectiveness of agriculture and forestry duly rose to the top of the agenda in a series of European states. British agriculture and Prussian techniques of rational forest management proved to be two parallel ideals in the early nineteenth century. Swedish developments, with the sprawling utilitarianism of the Age of Freedom, followed by an exaggerated faith in British agriculture during the Gustavian period, fit well with Scott's description, although it would be going too far to say that the sole reason for either was a fiscal determination to increase the tax base.

During the period in question, society, like its landscape, consisted of a multitude of local and regional customs, norms, methods, cultivation systems, traditions and livelihoods while local ecosystems, crops, and forms of animal husbandry were equally varied. Seen in light of the authorities' aims—to increase resource exploitation so as to strengthen society and the State—society and landscape alike were largely illegible. Of course, it is possible to imagine local systems of control and taxation that could keep track of every small-scale element of supply. However, from Scott's perspective, the authorities did not pursue this path, and instead created a choice; as far as they were concerned, only a few of these traditions and processes were of interest, in the sense of being able to contribute to an increase in resource exploitation. This was where agriculture came in; but only in those activities one could control.

For the authorities' part, it was of no interest whether more intractable forms of commerce played an important role in the local economy. Legibility therefore involved a powerfully reduced definition of reality to the detriment of those who lived and worked in rural communities. Legibility was a filter through which only a few forms of economic activity could pass. Multiple livelihoods, fishing, hunting, and commercial travel—all may have contributed to peasant households' upkeep. However, they were irrelevant from the authori-

---

21 This and the two subsequent paragraphs draw on Scott (1998, ch. 1; for legibility 22–24).

ties' perspective. It was this filter that led the authors of place descriptions to assert that travelling trade accustomed the peasantry to indolence and made them unsuitable for "real" work. Business travel was not work; tending to a farm was.[22] In other contexts, it was this filter that meant that the grand men of scientific agriculture failed to see the extensive use the peasantry made of Sweden's moorland, for they saw only one conceivable way forward, namely the destruction of the moor by converting it into farmland. The fishing and hunting that would be ruined in the process were only ruined for users; for the authorities, they never had existed in the first place.

It was very likely the case that the further from government one got—physically, as in Lapland or the remote forest districts; or socially, at the poorest margins of society (or both)—the less one's activities made it through the authorities' filter. This is something I think is demonstrated by Orvar Löfgren's study of the fishing community in Värö in Halland. There, the households of the poor were organized around a series of apparently irrelevant economic activities, and it is only when viewed in their entirety that a picture emerges of how they made a living. Seen in isolation, they appeared to live on nothing at all. There was nothing to be taxed or controlled—so much so that Löfgren notes that Värö's poor and landless lived wholly outside the official machinery's control system (Löfgren 1977, 55). He calls them "Jacks of all trades" (Löfgren 1977, 56). Contemporaries called them slackers ("lättingar" derived from the word *lättja*).

Legibility and Mobility, or the Art of Avoiding Control

Is it possible that the spatial aspect is an important factor in the legibility of society? Hypothetically, the more mobile something or someone is, the harder it will be to include in the realm of the legible. Scott has also asserted elsewhere that states and social elites in general always attempt to subjugate any and all who are mobile and to bind them to specific places. And why not? If one were utterly destitute, a Jack-Of-All-Trades at the very bottom of the Swedish agrarian community, then perhaps one had every possible reason to avoid appearing on the State's radar.

When considering the case for the authorities' legibility filter, it should not be forgotten that local communities may not have been mere victims, and could instead have used it to their own advantage. Here the Russian agrarian historian Boris Gorschkova's account of events in Yaroslavl in 1877 is of some

---

22 A clear example is Allvin (1937, 273–274), published in 1846.

help. A merchant and former serf was writing his memoirs. Farming methods in his own village were described as ineffective. His case is an example of how the serfs in the village were uninterested in running the farms. Contemporary observers would have regarded this as a standard example of a common peasant failing: the often discussed peasant routine, or peasant conservatism, meaning their inability to do anything differently from what their fathers and grandfathers had done. Yet the writer of the memoir believed that this was far from the case. He emphasized instead that it would have been stupid for the villagers to try to make a profit from farming, since their earnings were always taken from them by the landowners. Instead, the villagers spent time in other economic activities, hidden from the State and the authorities, or at least hard to trace. Gorschkov uses this autobiography to emphasize how common this strategy was in Russia: the serfs preferred to spend their time working in the towns or in the forests. Landowners could easily supervise agriculture and obtain a clear and accurate picture of their yields and profits; what they could not do was to keep an eye on what took place beyond the village's fields (Gorschkov 2000, 632). Öhrströmer, the priest on Väddö, comes to mind, with the thistle-choked fields of his parishioners. For a parish priest—who derived his salary from the peasants' work—the fields could be kept under continual surveillance. What he could not keep track of was what his parishioners were fishing from the sea.

The peasants' keen interest in non-farming activities was thus probably prompted by the fact that they could not be as effectively supervised and taxed (Gorshkov 2000, 632). Gorschkov here makes the obvious point that the authorities and citizens regard the benefit of different sorts of work in different ways. The citizens are mostly concerned with their own benefit, their own livelihoods. The authorities are concerned to an equally high degree with *their* own benefit, but, unlike the citizens, often have the rhetorical privilege of being able to clothe it terms of the public good. Ultimately, it revolved around conflicts over each community's resources. Lapland, with its intensifying competition for local resources between coastal farmers, settlers, and the indigenous Sami people, is the closest we can come in Sweden to Scott's South Asian example. Lennart Lundmark has shown how in the eighteenth and early nineteenth centuries the central government and its representatives at the county level always regarded agriculture and fixed habitation as fundamental. The local courts could act differently, above all by defending Sami claims to land and to hunting and fishing rights (Lundmark 2008, 66–71). Using a number of well-chosen examples, Lundmark has also shown how the population of Lapland used the differing sets of rules and regulations to avoid scrutiny and taxation. According to the rhetoric of the day, settlers in Lapland had chosen an easy path rather than work the land by the sweat of their brows.

It should be noted that hunting and fishing were in fact already subject to taxation; they were part of the Lapp Tax, the relatively insignificant tax paid by the Sami (but not the settlers) to the Crown (Lundmark 2008, 34, 66–67). Many observers noted that some settlers set out to exploit the system, first obtaining the formal title to newly settled land (which was tax-free for a number of years on condition that it was cultivated) and then instead of farming, using the land for fishing and hunting, even though it was only the Sami who paid taxes for the right to fish and hunt (Lundmark 2008, 92). These settlers were obviously developing the skills treated by Scott (2009) in his latest study of governmental vision: *The Art of NOT Being Governed*, or the art of remaining illegible to the state and therefore outside its ken. It is probably the necessity of being a Jack-of-All-Trades that Berch, Hülphers, Læstadius, and Sandman were thinking of when they complained of peasants wasting their days in the woods. Where these authors saw indolence, perhaps we should see peasants avoiding heavy manual work with low returns and high levels of exploitation. In other words, where the elite's ability to control society and raise taxes faltered, the rhetoric of indolence took over (Scott 2009, especially ix–xi).[23]

---

23 For the formulation that rhetoric takes over when control fails, of which this is a very free paraphrase, see Scott (2009, ix).

References

Adolfsson, Maria. 2000. *Fäderneslandets kännedom. Om svenska ortsbeskrivnings-projekt och ämbetsmäns folklivsskildringar under 1700- och 1800-talet.* Stockholm: Etnologiska institutionen, Stockholms universitet.

Allvin, Jonas. 1937. *Beskrifning öfver Wästbo Härad i jönköpings län. Nytryck av den 1846 utgivna originalupplagan.* Värnamo: Värnamo Nyheter.

Aspelin, David. 1810. *Anteckningar om Värends Härad i Småland. Första häftet.* Jönköping: Joh. P. Lundström.

Barchaeus, Anders Gustaf. 1924. *Underrättelser angående landthushållningen i Halland.* Lund: Gleerup.

Berch, Anders. 1747. *Inledning Til Almänna Hushålningen, Innefattande Grunden Til* Politie, Oeconomie, *Och* Cameral Wetenskaperne. Stockholm: Lars Salvius.

Berch, Anders (præses), Carl Fjellström (respondent). 1760. *Tankar om upod-lings möjelighet i Lapmarkerne.* Stockholm.

Berch, Anders (præses), Nordholm, Aeschill (respondent). 1953. *Jämtelands djur-fänge.* Tandbyn (1749).

Bernhardt, Gustaf. 1818. *Beskrifning öfwer Hardemo Socken uti Nerike.* Sträng-näs: Carl Erik Ekmarck.

Bexell, Sven Peter. 1817–19. *Hallands Historia och Beskrifning,* 3 vols. Göteborg: Sam. Norberg.

Carleson, Carl. 1759. *Tal Om spanmåls-bristens afhjelpande.* Stockholm: Lars Salvius.

Edelstam, G. 1816. "Uppgifter från Westerbottens Län, till Upplysning om Landthushållningens tillstånd derstädes, i anledning af Kongl. Landt-bruks-Academiens derom framställda frågor." *Kong. Svenska Landtbruks-Academiens Annaler,* 29–43.

Fiebranz, Rosemarie. 2002. *Jord, linne eller träkol? Genusordning och hushållsstrat-egier, Bjuråker 1750–1850.* Uppsala: Acta universitatis upsaliensis.

Fischerström, Johan. 1761a. "Anmärkningar Om Södra Halland." *Kongl. Sven-ska Vetenskaps Academiens Handlingar* 1761, no. 3–4: 230–242, 258–280.

———. 1761b. *Påminnelser wid Sweriges Allmänna och enskylta Hushållning.* Stockholm: Lorens Ludvig Grefing.

———. 1769. *Tal til det Svenska Folket år 1769.* Uppsala: Johan Edman.

Gestrich, Jonas. 1817. "Berättelse om Landthushållningens närvarande till-stånd i Jemtland, meddelad i anledning af Kongl. Landtbruks-Academiens begäran i Protocolls-Utdrag af den 18 October 1814." *Kongl. Svenska Landt-bruks-Academiens Annaler,* 142–163.

Gorshkov, Boris B. 2000. "Serfs on the Move: Peasant Seasonal Migration in Pre-Reform Russia, 1800–61." *Kritika: Explorations in Russian and Eurasian History* 1, no. 4: 627–656.

Helander, Adolf. 2001. *Beskrifning öfver Frölunda Socken i Askims Härad af Götheborgs Län.* Göteborg: Västra Fröunda Hembygdsförening. .

Hellberg, Johan Fredrik. 1824. *Försök till beskrifning öfver Orousts och Tjörns Häraders fögderier uti Götheborgs- och Bohus-Län.* Göteborg: Löwegren.

Hesselgren, Magnus. 1823. "Åhs och Kållerstads Socknar i Wedbo Härad." *Jönköpings Läns K:gl. Hushållnings-Sällskaps Handlingar, 118–154.*

Hielmquist, And. 1823. "Om Refteleds Pastorat." *Jönköpings Läns K:gl. Hushållnings-Sällskaps Handlingar, 154–176.*

Hülphers, Abraham. 1922. *Samlingar til en Beskrifning öfwer Norrland. Femte samlingen 3. Bandet om Lappmarken.* Stockholm: Norstedts.

Jonsson, Inger. 1994. *Linodlare, väverskor och köpmän. Linne som handlingsvara och försörjningsmöjlighet i det tidiga 1800-talets Hälsingland.* Uppsala: Acta universitatis upsaliensis.

Justelius, Claes. 1957. *Beskrifning öfver Täby 1813.* Roslags Näsby: Täby hembygdsförening.

Kihlman, Lars Fredrik. 1828. "Beskrifning öfver Kumla Socken." *Westmanlands Läns Kongl. Hushållningssällskaps Handlingar.*

Koselleck, Reinhart. 1972. "Einleitung." In *Geschichtliche Grundbegriffe: Historisches Lexikon zur Politisch-sozialen Sprache in Deutschland,* I. Stuttgart: Clett-Cotta.

Kryger, Johan Fredrik. 1758. *Tal Om Folkbristens Orsaker, Verkan och Hjelp.* Stockholm: Lars Salvius.

Laestadius, Lars Levi. 1981. *Om uppodlingar i Lappmarken på det allmännas bekostnad, jemte Förslag till en nybyggarscholas anläggande derstädes, eller anvisning, att på allmän bekostnad befrämja allmänna uppodlingar i nämnde landskap, till båtnad för staten.* Luleå: Tornedalica.

Lagergren, Jon. Fab. 1822. "Anteckningar rörande Tofteryds Pastorat." *Jönköpings Läns K:gl. Hushållnings-Sällskaps Handlingar, 168–182.*

Lamér, Magnus. 1815. "Allmän öfwersigt af landthushållningens tillstånd i Kronobergs Län: med anledning af underrättelser, som genom afgifne swar på framstälde frågor, af Sockne Hushållnings-Komitteerne benäget blifwit meddelade." *Kongl. Hushållnings-Sällskaps Handlingar, 34–48.*

Lindskog, Petter. 1985. *Försök till en korrt beskrifning om Skara Stift.* Ed: C. Zakariasson.

Löfgren, Orvar, *Fångstmän i industrisamhället. En halländsk kustbygds omvand-
ling 1800–1970*. Lund: LiberLäromedel.

Lundell, Jan. 2005. "Hur lönsamt var 'hälsingelinet'." *Hälsingerunor. En hem-
bygdsbok*, 59–84.

Lundmark, Lennart. 2008. *Stulet land: svensk makt på samisk mark*. Stockholm:
Ordfront.

[Mirabeau, Victor de Riquetti]. 1759. *Tankar om sedernas werkan på folk-mängden i et land*. Stockholm: Lars Salvius.

Montelin, Nils Johan. 2007. "Beskrifning öfver Järsnäs Socken, Upprättad År
1835." *Järsnäs Sockenbok*, Järsnäs: Järsnäs hembygdsförening, 62–71.

Næslund, Olof Emanuel. 1945. *Sockenbeskrivningar från Medelpad utgivna av
Arvid Enqvist*. In *Ol. Em. Næslund: Njuranda pastorat*. Sundsvall: Det Gamla
Medelpad.

Nordin, Daniel. 1827. "Beskrifning öfwer Wilstads Pastorat." *Jönköpings Läns
K:gl. Hushålnings-Sällskaps Handlingar*, 140–173.

Odencrants, Thor August. 1818. *Försök till Beskrifning öfwer Ljungarums Socken i
Jönköpings Län*. S.J. Westberg.

Öhrströmer, Fredrik. 1962. *Väddö socken 1801. Med levnadsbeskrivning och några
kommentarer utgiven i nytryck av Edvin Gustavsson*. Uppsala.

Radloff, Fredric Wilhelm. 1983. *Beskrifning öfver Roslagen. Norrtälje (first publ. as
Beskrifning öfver norra delen af Stockholms län, 2 vols., 1804–1805)*. Norrtälje:
Norrtälje tidning.

Rask, Sven. 1991. "Något om salpetersjudningen i Sverige." *Polhem. Tidskrift för
teknikhistoria*, 9 (3): 278–294.

Richter. Melvin. 1995. *The History of Political and Social Concepts: A critical introduction*. New York: Oxford University Press.

Runefelt, Leif. 2008. "Svensk mosskultur som överhetsprojekt före 1886." in
id. (ed.), *Svensk Mosskultur. Odling, torvanvändning och landskapets förändring
1750–2000*. Stockholm: Kungl. Skogs- och Lantbruksakademien, 27–52.

———. 2011. *En idyll försvarad. Ortsbeskrivningar, herrgårdskultur och den gamla
samhällsordningen*. Lund: Sekel Bokförlag.

Sandman, Esaias. 1941. "Lockne." In *Sockenbeskrivningar från Jämtland och Härje-
dalen 1818–1821, insända till Jämtlands kungl. hushållningssällskap*. Östersund:
Jämtlands läns fornskriftsällskap, 57–96.

S[chultze], S[amuel] T[homasson]. 1778. *Den swenske fiskaren eller Wälment
underrättelse om det i Sverige nu för tiden brukeliga fiskeri jemte beskrifning på de
bekanta fiskar och fiskeredskap*. Stockholm: Kongl. Tryckeriet.

Schönbeck, Christian. 1818. "Försök till Beskrifning öfwer Riseberga Socken. År 1817." *Handlingar af Christianstads Läns Kongl. Hushålls-Sällskap*, 31–59.

Scott, James C. 1998. *Seeing like a State. How certain Schemes to Improve the Human Condition have Failed*. New Haven: Yale University Press.

—. 2009. *The Art of Not Being Governed: An Anarchist History of Upland Southeast Asia*. New Haven: Yale University Press.

Sefström, Anders Gustaf. 1984. *Försök till en ekonomisk statistisk beskrivning öfwer Bjuråkers församling, författadt år 1816*. Bjuråker: Bjuråkers hembygdsförening.

Stiernström, Mårten Rikard. 1959. "Beskrifning öfver Själevads Socken i Westernorrlands Län och N:ra Ångermanland upprättad i enlighet med Kongl. Maj:ts nådiga bref af den 12 Dec. 1845 angående Socken-kartor." In *Själevad förr och nu 1*. Örnsköldsvik: Själevads hembygdsförening, 21–62.

Ström, Carl Petter. 1964. *Försök till en Beskrifning öfver Färla Socken*. Stockholm: Fabel.

Sylvén, Karl. 1929. *Beskrivning över Kristianopels socken. Författad åren 1854, 55 och 56 av Karl Sylvén, kommissionslantmätare i Blekinge län. Meddelad av Pehr Johnsson*. Karlskrona.

Utterström, Gustaf. 1957. *Jordbrukets arbetare. Levnadsvillkor och arbetsliv på landsbygden från frihetstiden till mitten av 1800-talet*, 2 vols. Stockholm: Tiden.

Wahlenberg, Göran. 1804. *Geografisk och ekonomisk beskrifning om Kemi Lappmark i Vesterbottens Höfdingdöme. Med geografisk karta*. Stockholm: Carl Delén.

Westerman, Johan. 1768. *Inträdes-tal, Om Svenska Näringarnes Undervigt emot de Utländske, förmedelst en trögare Arbetsdrift*. Stockholm: Lars Salvius.

Wibelius, Gustaf. 1849. *Beskrifning öfver Tredje Fögderiet af Uppsala Län. Lagunda, Hagunda och Ulleråkers Härader*. Stockholm.

A Post-Holocaust Philosopher of Forgiveness: An Exploration of Hannah Arendt's Jesus

Abstract

This paper examines Hannah Arendt's image of Jesus. While Arendt's drawing on Jesus was unusual in political theory, her depiction of Jesus was on a number of points homologous with some theological research into the historical Jesus. Like the theologians, Arendt presented the teaching of Jesus as unique and unprecedented. Additionally, to associate Jesus' uniqueness with forgiveness is obviously a "theological commonplace." Yet, unlike the prevailing eschatological image of Jesus, Arendt portrayed Jesus as an ethical-political sage. In this regard, her portrayal had more in common with a previous "Jesus paradigm" which highlighted the morality and humanity of Jesus. Moreover, the quality of what she identified as Jesus' unprecedented insight was unorthodox. Thus, "Arendt's Jesus" insisted that forgiveness is a purely human action, i.e., that humans have the capacity to forgive and that this capacity is not derived from God. Furthermore, whereas Jesus is commonly associated with an unlimited power to forgive, Arendt's Jesus maintained that forgiveness does not apply to deliberate wrongdoing and emphasized that some wrongdoers are unforgivable. In this regard, Arendt drew a post-Holocaust image of Jesus. The paper concludes that Arendt's image is "ambivalent," because, on one hand, Arendt's Jesus considered forgiveness to be an extraordinary human power. On the other hand, he was a proponent of a highly circumscribed forgiveness. Beyond this, the relationship between Arendt's Jesus and her political thought is considered. It is contended that Arendt's "alliance" with Jesus is strategic. This in that it functions as a part of her critique of the Western tradition of political thought for being biased and out of tune with elementary human experiences and conditions.

* Thomas Ø. Wittendorff is doctoral researcher, Department of History and Civilization, European University Institute.

Introduction

The German-American philosopher Hannah Arendt (1906-75) introduced to political theory a highly eccentric and non-traditional "theorist": Jesus of Nazareth. Her appealing to Jesus was connected to another unconventional contention: that forgiveness should constitute a central part of political theory.[1] Famously—and questionably—she claimed that Jesus was the "discoverer of the role of forgiveness in the realm of human affairs" (Arendt 1989, 238). Arendt's project was, as she put it, "to take seriously" Jesus' teaching in "a strictly secular sense" (Arendt 1989, 238). Hence, in support of her outline for a political and non-religious clarification of forgiveness, Arendt called on one of the world's most religiously loaded figures.

While Arendt's positive assessment of Jesus has often been noted, there has been no exploration of how, more specifically, she depicted Jesus or of how her depiction related to other images of Jesus.[2] Thus, despite the fact that Arendt is a major figure in twentieth century intellectual history and that she refers repeatedly to Jesus, there are no separate studies of this aspect of her thought. The aim of this paper is to begin to rectify this.[3] In addition to comparing her depiction with the historiography of Jesus, it will be considered how it relates to and serves her political thought and theory of action. Rather than entering into a discussion of the validity of Arendt's interpretation or addressing its historically problematic aspects, the aim is to explore the picture of Jesus drawn by Arendt. It should be noted that even though Arendt referred to Jesus as a historical person, she treated Jesus ahistorically in the sense that she ignored the critical question as to what extent and on what basis a reconstruction of the historical Jesus is possible. Having entered academia as a student of theology, Arendt was not ignorant of the existence of this intricate and historical problem. Instead, it indicates that Arendt did not intend to contribute to the historical research into the person of Jesus. This

---

1 One is to bear in mind that when Arendt made this case in the 1950s, forgiveness had not yet become a cross-disciplinary theme.

2 E.g. Kateb (1984, 26, 89) talks about Arendt's "amazing meditation on Jesus" and observes that she "has a startling reverence for the figure of Jesus," and Bernstein (1996, 185) states that Arendt "wrote with great insight and feeling about Jesus of Nazareth." See also Canovan (1995, 179ff); Gottlieb (2003, 154).

3 The paper, accordingly, focuses on the intersection of Arendt's writings on forgiving and on Jesus. While there are no separate studies of Arendt's image of Jesus, there are a number of works on her reflections on forgiveness. There is, however, only one monograph: Dürr (2009). Other important works include: Hagedorn (2007), Pullich (1999). The English literature on this particular subject is, in my estimation, of a lower quality, partly for the rather remarkable reason that it does not engage with the extensive German literature on the subject. Recommendable, though, is Young-Bruehl (2009).

does not affect what is at issue in this paper: that she, like the theological-historical explorations, depicted an image of Jesus. It is precisely this which is of particular relevance in the present study—that Jesus is, *par excellence,* an object of projections. If it is questionable how much the various Jesus portrayals actually say about Jesus, it is a well-established fact that they reveal a great deal about the authors themselves and their time.[4]

Aside from being brief and sporadic, the remarks on Arendt's depiction of Jesus can often be considered misinterpretations. A prominent example of this can be found in one of the standard works on Arendt's thought: Margaret Canovan's *Hannah Arendt: A Reinterpretation of Her Political Thought.* In her distinguished book, Canovan (1995, 179) contends that "Arendt took for granted a 'demythologised' view of Jesus according to which he was not God incarnate but a unique and extraordinary man." The term "demythologizing" (*Entmythologisierung*) denotes a certain hermeneutic approach to the New Testament which was developed by Arendt's theological teacher at Marburg University, the internationally acclaimed New Testament scholar Rudolf Bultmann. However, the association of Arendt's approach to and image of Jesus with Bultmann's is profoundly misleading. The view of Jesus as a unique and extraordinary human is in fact associated with nineteenth century liberal theology—and it is a view which Bultmann (1988, 18) explicitly opposes.[5] Another example is Susannah Gottlieb (2003, 154) who proposes that Arendt's interpretation of Jesus is situated within a German-Jewish tradition of scholarship on Jesus which ran from Abraham Geiger (1810–74) to Martin Buber (1878–1965).[6] In consideration of Arendt's Jewish background, this is potentially a reasonable suggestion. Unfortunately, however, Gottlieb does not substantiate her suggestion. It turns out that it does not stand up to scrutiny, because in fact the differences between Arendt and this tradition are more evident than the similarities. While the scholars of this tradition are sympathetic to Jesus, their identification with him is based on their insistence on his Jewishness. Thus, the theory of the founder of this tradition, Geiger, was that Jesus was a Pharisee, and that he taught nothing fundamentally new (Heschel 1998). Arendt (1989, 239), by contrast, stresses the uniqueness of

---

4 That writings on Jesus tend to be cultural and historical mirrors of their authors was observed already by Schweitzer in 1906; see below.

5 As we shall see, Bultmann was a leading proponent of the view that it is impossible to reconstruct the historical Jesus. Canovan (1995, 179), moreover, states that Karl Jaspers subscribed to the demythologizing approach; but Jaspers was in fact one of the harshest critics of Bultmann (see Jaspers and Bultmann [1954]).

6 For an exposition of this tradition, see Heschel (1998).

Jesus and presents Jesus as arguing "against the scribes and Pharisees," and she does not comment on the Jewishness of Jesus. Hence, Arendt stands out by sidestepping, or by showing a lack of interest in, this question.

Canovan and Gottlieb are exceptional in that they attempt to relate Arendt to other scholarly works on Jesus: the tendency in the commentary literature is to present Arendt's drawing on Jesus as being altogether unprecedented and *one of a kind*. For example, Elisabeth Young-Bruehl (2009, 61) states that "there had been no precedent for drawing upon the thought of Jesus of Nazareth as a historical person and a political sage—not, as the theologians of that time held, a herald of the apocalypse and retribution for human sinfulness." This, it will be argued, is an exaggeration of how singular Arendt's approach to Jesus was; it describes her interpretation as being totally exceptional—as if it were wholly unrelated to the historiography of Jesus. Undoubtedly, the prevailing image of Jesus was apocalyptic and eschatological. Yet this was by no means the case with the previous "Jesus paradigm." In fact, liberal theology, as it developed in the nineteenth century, drew on Jesus as a historical person and presented him as an ethical teacher. This is of course not to say that Arendt should be considered a liberal theologian; rather, it is to point out that there are some parallels between Arendt and this tradition concerning the specific question of "Jesus construal." Arendt's way of drawing on Jesus can only be understood as being unprecedented if one views it from an "isolated" political theory perspective.

I. Arendt's Jesus

Arendt assumed that the teachings of Jesus had been misrepresented in the Christian tradition, beginning already with Paul.[7] The center of Paul's teaching, Arendt (1978, 65) maintained, "is not Jesus of Nazareth, his preaching and his deeds, but Christ, crucified and resurrected." Hence, "when we come to Paul, the accent shifts entirely from doing to believing;" from the outward humans of action and plurality to an inwardness and introspection concerned with the individual's salvation from the world (Arendt 1978, 67; cf. 1989, 8;

---

7 Yet in her 1928 dissertation, *Der Liebesbegriif bei Augustin,* Arendt sees Paul as representing genuine Christianity (Arendt 1996b). While Arendt changes her mind on the question as to whether Paul represents or betrays original and authentic Christianity, she presents in either case the betrayal as resulting from contamination by the otherworldly and contemplative priority of the Greek metaphysical tradition. Regarding juxtaposing Jesus with Paul, this became common during the nineteenth century, notably not only among rebels and outsiders like Nietzsche and Kierkegaard, but also among influential historical theologians. See Furnish (1965).

Dürr 2009, 43–44).[8] Christianity "as a religion, as an institution in this world," claims Arendt (1973), "was not founded by Jesus. It was founded by those who believed in Jesus as Christ. That is, it was founded by Paul."

In Arendt's view, the Church's teachings were thus not what Jesus taught. In her rendition of Jesus, Arendt sought to reach behind what she saw as a worn-out tradition in order to gain access to the authentic experiences from which the tradition originated, that is, the authentic teachings of Jesus. As a result, one needs to be aware that there is a distinction in Arendt's writings between Jesus' teachings and the Christian traditions (Arendt 1973; 1989, 74ff; 1970, 81–95; cf. Canovan 1995, 179–185).[9] Arendt bases her account of the authentic teachings of Jesus on the Gospels. As mentioned, she is "deliberately unscholarly" and ahistorical in that she leaves out of concern the source-critical question as to what extent the Gospels can be regarded as historically reliable representations of Jesus.[10]

Arendt's strategy of "immanent critique"—of using traditional sources against the tradition—can, as several scholars have observed, be seen as an employment of Heidegger's so-called *destruction* approach.[11] In terms of the more specific question of Arendt's approach to Jesus and her distinction between the historical Jesus and the dogmatic and "institutionalized" Christ, it should be noted, however, that this was a very common thought mode. Notably, it was so among Christian thinkers too; especially, as we shall see, among historically minded liberal theologians. Also, it was very common to "reserve the criticism" for institutionalized Christianity, while being "unreservedly positive" when it comes to Jesus. In fact, this applies also to anti-Christian thinkers; even Nietzsche, in the midst of his curse (*Fluch*) of Christianity in *The Anti-Christ* (1888), is sympathetic to Jesus. Thus, for liberal theologians and for critics of religion alike, the distinction between the true, historical Jesus and the "dogmatically distorted" Christ was interrelated with an anti-

---

8 In section two, we shall return to Arendt's notion of action and plurality, and her linking it to Jesus.

9 See also the letter that Arendt sent to her friend, the famous Protestant theologian Paul Tillich, upon the publication of *The Human Condition*; here, Arendt stresses that she draws on "Jesus, not Christ" (Christophersen and Schulze 2002, 145).

10 In the scholarly literature, the Gospels' accounts of the "earthly Jesus" are regarded as theologically guided narratives, and it is a highly complex and debated question which parts of their accounts, if any, that are historically reliable. Arendt, more precisely, bases her interpretation on the Synoptic Gospels, i.e., Mark, Matthew, and Luke. This resembles the "Life of Jesus-genre" of nineteenth century liberal theology; see below.

11 The relationship—intellectual as well as personal—between Arendt and Heidegger is heavily studied. For an exploration of Arendt's ways of employing Heidegger's destruction approach, see Villa (1996, 159ff); Gordon (2007, 71–72).

institutional interpretation of Jesus. This is indeed the case for Arendt too. Jesus, Arendt contends, "did not know what institutions are," and his teachings are characterized by a "strong anti-institutional tendency" (Arendt 1973; 2005, 50). Whereas Arendt criticizes Christianity on a number of points—her most profound accusation being that it is anti-political and other-worldly in its focus—her assessment of Jesus is unambiguously and overwhelmingly positive.[12] What is in focus here is solely Arendt's account of Jesus.

Arendt is preoccupied with identifying the uniqueness and originality of the human being Jesus of Nazareth, which, as we shall see, is similar to liberal theological-historical research into the historical Jesus. Accordingly, she uses phrases that echo this tradition, such as the "originality and unprecedentedness" of Jesus' teaching, the "novelty in Jesus' teaching," "the preaching and living example of Jesus of Nazareth," and the "unique conclusion that Jesus of Nazareth drew" (Arendt 1989, 247, 240; 2005, 56, 58; cf. 2003, 124). Moreover, like the theological studies, the "level of uniqueness" which Arendt ascribes to Jesus is extremely high, using expressions such as the "only... experience Western mankind had ever had" (Arendt 2006, 72). She declares Jesus to be nothing less than the first person in world history to acknowledge "the role of forgiveness in the realm of human affairs" (Arendt 1989, 238; see also 2003, 89). In this regard, Arendt actually reflects a defining part of Christian self-image: that Christianity—as opposed to other religions, especially in contrast to the Jewish religion from which it developed—is *the* religion of forgiveness, and Christians are those who forgive. Yet, in her linking of Jesus' "discovery" to "the realm of human affairs" and "the nature of human action itself," Arendt is unconventional (Arendt 1989, 238; 2005, 57). In other words, she is unconventional when it comes to the quality of the uniqueness she identifies in Jesus.

The core of what Arendt sees as an unprecedented insight in Jesus' teaching consists, more specifically, of two interrelated aspects. First is that not only God, but humans as well, are capable of forgiving, or, in Arendt's (1989, 238) formulation, have "the power to forgive." In other words, Jesus "went so far as to deny explicitly that forgiving is the sole prerogative of God" (Arendt

---

12 The question of Arendt's view of and relationship with Christianity is a complex and contested one. At the one end of the interpretative spectrum, Moyn (2008, 75) presents Arendt as "a thinker who is uninterested in or opposed to religion in general and Christianity in particular." At the other end of the spectrum, we find scholars such as the contributors to an anthology on Arendt edited by the Jesuit philosopher James Bernauer (1987; cf. Bernauer 2007), who depict Arendt as being very sympathetic to Christianity, without going quite as far, though, as Schanz (2007, 63) who bluntly appoints Arendt to be "one of the greatest Christian philosophers of the twentieth century."

2005, 57). Second, the human capacity to forgive "does not derive from God" (Arendt 1989, 239).[13] Actually, "Jesus' formulation is even more radical," Arendt advances; forgiveness is "primarily a human power" insofar as humans must first practice forgiveness of each other before "they can hope to be forgiven by God also" (Arendt 1989, 239). That is, humans are not supposed to forgive each other because God forgives and they "must do likewise;" on the contrary, God forgives humans their debts, as they have also forgiven their debtors, Arendt (1989, 239) argues with reference to the Lord's Prayer: "For if you forgive men their trespasses, your heavenly Father will also forgive you. But if you do not forgive men their trespasses, neither will your Father forgive your trespasses" (Matt. 6:14–15). Hence, in Arendt's reading, Jesus proposed that divine forgiveness is dependent on the human power to forgive, or as she puts it; he "dared to think that God's mercy for the sins of men may ultimately depend upon man's willingness to forgive the trespasses of the others" (Arendt 2005, 57). This challenge of God's prerogative or "forgiveness monopoly" is, according to Arendt, essentially what sets Jesus apart from contemporary Judaism and what provokes opposition and hostility.

The heart of the uniqueness of "Arendt's Jesus" is thus that he revealed that forgiveness is "a strictly human action" (Arendt 2005, 59). This concerns the question of the authority of forgiveness or, in Arendt's terminology, of who has the "power to forgive." Another question is that of the scope and limits of forgiveness; and on this point, too, Arendt takes an unconventional stand. Whereas Jesus is commonly associated with an unlimited power of forgiveness, "Arendt's Jesus" is a proponent of a limited and confined concept of forgiveness, hence placing much under the category of the unforgivable. Thus, Arendt stresses that Jesus' "command to forgive is not unconditional" and that there are perpetrators whom it is "beyond the power to forgive." (1960a; Arendt's underlining). More precisely, it is Arendt's claim that Jesus distinguished between *trespassing* and *offence*. The former is transgressions that "we are confronted with daily and with which we know how to come to terms or how to get rid of," since Jesus teaches us that we "are supposed to forgive [the agents of trespassing] 'seven times a day'" (Arendt 2003, 109; cf. 1989, 239; Luke 17:4). *Trespassing* is Arendt's translation of the New Testament Greek term *hamartanein*. It means, notes Arendt (1989, 240), "rather

13 That this is unconventional and theologically controversial is attested by the reception of Arendt in the theological literature. While theologians generally embrace Arendt's depiction of Jesus as "forgiveness discoverer," a common attempt in their comments is to refute Arendt's claim that inter-human forgiveness is not derived from God (see e.g. Scheiber (2006); Wolterstorff (2008); Malcolm (2010); Waters (2010).

'to miss,' 'fail and go astray,' than 'to sin'." It is key to Arendt's interpretation, as these etymological comments indicate, that trespassing denotes *unintended* harm or, in other words, unwanted and unforeseen consequences of one's actions. Accordingly, the reason for Jesus' "insistence on a duty to forgive [humans who have trespassed] is clearly 'for they know not what they do'," Arendt (1989, 239; cf. 2005, 57) reasons, quoting the words that Luke ascribes to Jesus on the cross.[14] However, notably, this duty applies only to trespassing. Indeed, Arendt (1989, 237, 239) goes as far as to state that agents of trespassing not only did not know that their acts would have harmful consequences, but also could not have known it and even could not have avoided it. The concept of forgiveness that correlates with trespassing, consequently, has more in common with what is usually categorized as *excuse* than with forgiveness. The point here, however, is not to enter into conceptual analysis on the relationship between forgiveness and excuse, but merely to draw attention to the fact that the notion of forgiveness that Arendt finds in Jesus' teaching is highly circumscribed.

Most striking is it that evil is excluded from this concept of forgiveness—notably, not merely extreme forms of evil, but all kinds of deliberate wrongdoing, or what Arendt (1989, 240) calls "willed evil."[15] Arendt terms these deeds *offences*, which is her translation of the New Testament Greek word *skandala* (Arendt 1989, 240; cf. 2003, 109).[16] A *skandalon*, observes Arendt 2003, 109), "originally meant a trap laid for one's enemies and ... is used as the equivalent for the Hebrew word *mikhshol* or *zur mikhshol* which means 'stumbling block.'" An offence, accordingly, is like a stumbling block which "cannot be removed from our path;" it is something which it is "not in our power to repair," an "unsurmountable obstacle" (Arendt 2003, 125, 109f; cf. 1989, 240). However, not only is it something which "human powers cannot remove;" it cannot be forgiven by God either (Arendt 2003, 125). "[A]ccording to Jesus," Arendt

---

14 Luke 23:34: "And Jesus said, 'Father, forgive them, for they know not what they do.'"

15 As to Arendt's emphasis on intentionality, it should be pointed out that these reflections originate from the mid-1950s, i.e., before she, in her controversial reflections on the Eichmann trial, introduced the concepts of banal and rootless evil to describe a specific kind of totalitarian evil. With these concepts, Arendt attacked the assumption that evil doings presuppose evil motives: Eichmann, Arendt insisted, committed monstrous crimes without being driven by monstrous, evil intentions, but rather by banal intentions, such as carrier advancement (Arendt 2006c). In her book on Eichmann, Arendt did not consider if her new categories of evil had implications to her understanding of forgiveness; but it seems to imply that there is a part of the unforgivable which cannot be described as willed evil. Yet, it does not affect the scope of forgiveness, given that forgiveness addresses (the negative consequences of) action—and it is Arendt's remarkable claim that action, in her technical definition of the activity, is wholly detached from motives (be they banal or not); see below.

16 Arendt refers to Luke 17:2; cf. Mark 9:42; Matt 18:6.

(1989, 240) advances, perpetrators of deliberate evil "will be taken care of by God in the Last Judgment;" and as Arendt emphasizes (with reference to the statement in Matt 16:27 that everyone will be repaid or rewarded in keeping with their deeds), "the Last Judgment is not characterized by forgiveness, but by just retribution." Arendt here points to the tension in the New Testament between the notion of God's grace and forgiveness on one hand and of God's judgment on the other. Moreover, this can be seen as an anti-Lutheran dimension of Arendt's interpretation, or at least as a drawing attention to what is a sensitive subject for Protestant theology in general and Lutheran theology in particular: that the New Testament is pervaded by the idea of judgment. Lutheran theology has an antipathy to the idea of judgment; primarily for the reason that it indicates that human deeds determine humans' relationships to God. This is at odds with the Lutheran tenet of *sola fide*, of justification by faith alone, and of salvation not by human merits but, solely and undeservedly, by God's grace.[17] Furthermore, Arendt (1989, 240) insists that the Last Judgment "plays no role whatsoever in life on earth." If someone has committed an offence in "life on earth," the conclusion is severe: "we can indeed only repeat with Jesus: 'It were better for him that a millstone were hanged about his neck, and he cast into the sea'" (Arendt 1989, 241).[18] This is due to the fact that, when confronted with an offence, "all we can say is: This should never have happened" (Arendt 2003, 75; cf. 109). The agent of an offence is, "to take another of Jesus' metaphors," Arendt adds, "like the weed, 'the tares in the field,' with which one can't do anything except destroy them, burn them in the fire" (Arendt 2003, 125; cf. Matt. 13:24ff).

Now, that extermination should be the attitude towards agents of all sorts of willed evil appears to be exaggerated and out of proportion. Similarly, it is questionable whether intentional wrongdoing is as "rare" as Arendt (1989, 240) assumes, since it includes not only extreme evil but also, as it were, "minor deliberate wrongdoing." There are clear indications that what Arendt had in mind was solely the former; more specifically, genocide and totalitarian crimes against humanity. Thus, in her description of what she takes to be Jesus' notion of *scandala*, she uses several of the same formulations as she does in her characterization of totalitarianism. For instance, the sentence "this

---

17 If one is judged in keeping with one's deeds, one can, as it were, decide one's own salvation. For an outline of the notion of judgment and Judgment Day in the New Testament, and of the reluctance of Lutheran theology to it, see Hallbäck (2003, 136–137).

18 Cf. Luke 17:2; Mark 9:42; Matt 18:6. Arendt quotes this repeatedly; see also Arendt 1989, 239; 2005, 75, 109, 125; 1960a.

should never have happened" is key to her description of the Holocaust: "One had had the idea that everything in one way or another could be remedied. Not this. This should never have happened" (*Dies hätte nie geschehen dürfen*) (Arendt 1996a, 59).[19] Another example is that Arendt states that the agent of an offence is "an offender to the world order as such" (Arendt 2003, 125; cf. 1989, 241). Additionally, Arendt (2003, 126) points out the political and societal aspects of offences, as she maintains that Jesus with his notion of *skandala* "stressed ... the harm done to the community, the danger arising to all." All this indicates that what Arendt really had in mind with *offences* was totalitarian crimes, not all sorts of deliberate wrongdoing. Particularly, the fact that Arendt uses the very same wording in her characterization of offences as she does in her description of the Holocaust suggests that her image of Jesus is a post-Holocaust image of Jesus.

Moreover, Arendt (2003, 109) contends that "Jesus' distinction" between trespassing and offence indicates more than the traditional Catholic distinction between venial and mortal sins; it "indicates that these stumbling blocks [*scandala*] cannot be removed." Arendt does not explicate in what way, more precisely, it indicates more; but probably it is due to the fact that in the case of the so-called mortal sins, there are in fact prescripts of how to deal with them and how to get on.[20]

Insofar as an *offence* goes beyond traditional categories, it denotes something new and unprecedented—a "horrible novelty" (Arendt 1970, ix)—and yet, in expressing this novel insight, Arendt refers to Jesus. Probably, the explanation is that Arendt claims to detect an insight, so to speak, behind the tradition.

The conception of forgiveness which Arendt identifies in the teachings of Jesus thus appears to be very limited in scope. This has led Sigrid Weigel (2002) to contend that Arendt subjects forgiveness to a "normalization." The normalization is, according to Weigel, linked to secularization: unlike "a reli-

---

19 Quotations from non-English literature are my own translations.

20 An agent of a mortal sin is prescribed to confess and do penance in the sacrament of reconciliation by means of which (s)he will be able to receive forgiveness; only if (s)he does not do this will (s)he be condemned to hell. Interestingly, in determining whether a given sin is mortal or venial, a key criterion is the relation between will and act, that is, whether the wrongdoing was committed deliberately. Hence, in this regard the distinction of Arendt's Jesus is similar to the traditional one. In terms of the latter, however, this is not the sole criterion; it also takes into account the graveness of the wrongdoing. That is, in order for a wrongdoing to be classified as a mortal sin, it requires not only that it is committed with full knowledge and deliberate consent; it must also entail grave matters. For an overview of the notions of mortal and venial sins, see Colle (2011, 325, 529). Beyond this, it is worthy of note that Arendt does not mention that there is a similar categorization of wrongdoings in Jewish tradition. For a reflection on forgiveness and the Talmud, see Levinas (1990).

gious connotation," argues Weigel (2002, 320–321), Arendt holds that forgiveness "occurs in ... 'the common world.'" Weigel also asserts that Arendt
is "concerned with its anchoring in everyday action, resulting in the secularization of forgiveness." It is not quite clear, however, why this is unlike "a
religious connotation." Do religious interpretations, in other words, rule out
that forgiveness can occur in the common world and in everyday life? Does
that not depend on the type of religion? Moreover, while it is clear that it
can be characterized as a normalization, this characterization captures in
fact only one side of Arendt's conception. The qualities which Arendt's Jesus
discovered in forgiveness can by no means be designated as a normalization,
but are rather the opposite. Hence, Arendt praises "the freedom contained
in Jesus' teaching of forgiveness" which implies that humans "can be trusted
with so great a power as that to begin something new" and she even terms
forgiveness a "miracle" (Arendt 1989, 241, 240, 246).[21] This seems paradoxical. If forgiveness has such extraordinary qualities, why does it not possess a
greater forgiveness potentiality? Is there not a discrepancy between Arendt's
description of what forgiveness addresses and the extraordinary qualities she
ascribes to forgiveness?[22]

Finally, an aspect of forgiveness which Arendt (1989, 241) contends "was
clearly recognized by Jesus" is what she calls the "personal element" in forgiving. This denotes the idea that forgiveness is "directed solely to the person,
not the deed." It is, in other words, not the wrong, but the wrongdoer, who "is
the center of the act [of forgiving]" (Arendt 1960b, 237). Consequently, "I can
forgive somebody without forgiving anything; if I forgive a 'thing' then only
that I was wronged" (Arendt 1960a; cf. 1970, 248). This is, to cite another of
Arendt's formulations, due to the fact that "if a wrong is forgiven, then one
forgives the person who has committed it, which naturally does not in the
least change that the wrong was wrong [*daß das Unrecht unrecht war*]" (Arendt
1960b).[23] To substantiate her claim that the personal element of forgiveness

21 Miracle, in Arendt's "strictly secular" reading, signifies the human capacity, inherent in
forgiveness, of acting completely unexpectedly and, accordingly, beginning something new. See also
Arendt (2006, 166ff.).

22 This contrast in Arendt's conceptualization between the quality and addressee of forgiveness has
led another Arendt scholar, Schanz (2007, 50), to raise a diametrically opposite point of criticism
against Arendt: that she excludes the banal and familiar from forgiveness, thus neglecting that
forgiveness is not always of a "deep, existential kind." These opposite points of criticism can be
explained by the fact that whereas Weigel is concerned solely with what forgiveness addresses, Schanz
does not take this question into account, but focuses merely on the qualities which Arendt ascribes to
forgiveness.

23 This distinction which Arendt proposes between person and deed has become paradigmatic in the
current literature on forgiveness.

was recognized by Jesus, Arendt (1989, 241f) refers to Jesus' forgiveness of a sinful woman, as narrated in Luke 7:47: "Her sins which are many are for-given; for she loved much: but to whom little is forgiven, the same loveth little." As appears to be the case based on this narration, Jesus related the personal element in forgiveness to love; this is a source, argues Arendt, of what she takes to be the current, misguided conviction that forgiveness is exclusively connected to love, or in her wording, that "only love has the power to forgive" (Arendt 1989, 241; cf. 1970, 248). Arendt suggests that it is "the connection with love attending its [forgiveness'] discovery"—alongside the fact that Jesus made the discovery in a "religious context and articulated it in a religious language"—which is the main reason why forgiveness "has always been deemed unrealistic and inadmissible in the public realm" (Arendt 1989, 243, 238). Remarkably, this is the only point where Arendt "corrects" what she takes to be Jesus' conception of forgiveness. The reason for assuming that only love can forgive is, reasons Arendt (1989, 241), that it is the most eminently personal human phenomenon—that only love is "fully receptive" to the person. While Arendt concedes that love has an "unequalled power" to forgive, she criticizes the idea that forgiveness is exclusively connected to love. If this were the case, forgiveness would have been politically irrelevant. Love, in Arendt's limited definition, is an exceptional phenomenon which can exist solely in twosome relationships.[24] "Yet what love is in its own, narrowly circum-scribed sphere," advances Arendt (1989, 243), "respect is in the larger domain of human affairs. Respect, not unlike the Aristotelian *philia politikê*, is a kind of 'friendship' without intimacy." Given that respect, like love, "concerns only the person, [it] is quite sufficient to prompt forgiving of what a person did, for the sake of the person" (Arendt 1989, 243).[25] Forgiveness based on respect thus functions in the same way as forgiveness based on love. This is in the sense that it is also directed to the person. However, there is a marked differ-ence in the scope of forgiveness: whereas the political forgiveness that Arendt advocates is sharply delimited, love is inclined to forgive the beloved person

---

24 According to Arendt (1989, 51–52), love is "killed, or rather extinguished, the moment it is displayed in public." Because of this hiding character, Arendt (1989, 242) even designates love as "not only apolitical but antipolitical." Moreover, one is to bear in mind that love, in Arendt's terminology, is not to be confused with the Christian notion of charity (Arendt 1960a; 1989, 53, 74, 242). Arendt developed her criticism of charity (*Nächstenliebe*) already in her 1928 dissertation on St. Augustine's concept of love (Arendt 1996b). As we shall see, her analysis of love bears affinity to her analysis of goodness.

25 As Arendt does not relate this part of her theory to Jesus, we shall not expand on it; only, we shall note that friendship in the Aristotelian, political sense which Arendt employs the term is not based on knowing one another, but solely on an acknowledgement of each other as fellow humans.

"whatever he may have done" (Arendt 1989, 243; cf. 1960a). This aspect of Arendt's reflections on forgiveness, which she introduces towards the end of her section on forgiveness in *The Human Condition*, is surprising, considering that her prior emphasis has been the limits of forgiveness. With regard to Arendt's construal of Jesus, it raises the following critical question: if Jesus connected forgiveness to love, how, then, is it possible to present him as a proponent of a circumscribed, political concept of forgiveness?

II. The Relationship between Arendt's Jesus and Arendt's Political Thought

Arendt's appeals to Jesus should be understood as a part of her critique of the Western tradition of political philosophy for being out of tune with basic human experience. "It has been in the nature of our tradition of political thought," Arendt (1989, 238–239) contends, "to be highly selective and to exclude from articulate conceptualization a great variety of authentic political experiences." One example of this is "[c]ertain aspects of the teaching of Jesus of Nazareth," which "have been neglected because of their allegedly exclusively religious nature" (Arendt 1989, 239). Arendt instead insists that the fact that Jesus articulated his insight in a religious context does not imply that it cannot be of political significance (Arendt 1989, 238; cf. 2006, 166). Arendt's attempt to develop a political theory in correspondence with what she takes to be elementary human experiences and conditions involves tracing sources of "conceptual biases" and distortions. This is followed up by redefinitions of traditional political concepts, as well as introductions of some new concepts which, according to Arendt, have been neglected in political theory—a prime example being forgiveness. With this purpose in mind, Arendt exploits materials outside the canon of political philosophy. Notably, she does not only exploit philosophical texts but also figures and resources in the history of religion and theology as well as in literature, using these sources on equal terms in her political anthropology. For example, Arendt refers to the notion of Daimon in Greek mythology and to an insight in *Ecclesiastes* which "does not necessarily arise from specifically religious experience," just as she draws on a large number of poets, maintaining that literature should also be dealt with "from a political viewpoint" (Arendt 1989, 204; 1970, 210–211). Thus, Arendt is not only engaged in criticism of religion: she also constructively employs religious sources in her political theory.

When referring to the history of religion and to theological ideas, Arendt's aim is not to devise an interpretation wherein a religious proclamation can be valid on contemporary premises. Rather, she seeks to extract an elementary political insight which has been discovered in a religious context. As Arendt's project is universalistic, one could explain her goals as follows: she seeks to trace the historical origins of the recognitions of universal experiences, of experiences that constitute her political anthropology. Furthermore, as Weigel (2002, 321) points out, it is not that Arendt subscribes to a political theology, as coined by the (in)famous political and legal thinker Carl Schmitt in Arendt's formative years in Weimar Germany, according to which all significant political terms are secularized theological concepts.[26]

Arendt's alliance with Jesus can be read as a part of her critique of the tradition of political thought. She uses her depiction of Jesus as one of her strategies for rectifying and rethinking the political, for bringing it into accord with her account of human conditions and experiences. But how, more precisely, does Arendt's interpretation of Jesus serve her political theory and her theory of action? In order to assess this, a few introductory comments are required.

Briefly explained, Arendt's concept of action forms a part of her wideranging project, presented in *The Human Condition* (1958). This is to "think what we are doing," or conceptualize elementary conditions and experiences of humans' active life, the *vita activa* (Arendt 1989, 5). Arendt's overarching agenda is to "rehabilitate" *vita activa*. As she is highly critical of the ways in which it has been conceptualized, her project is "corrective." As mentioned, her accusation against the Western tradition is that it has generally failed to illuminate and acknowledge fundamental human realities and experiences. The main reason for this neglect is that contemplative life has been favored and regarded as a higher form of life. The "original sinner" in Arendt's narrative is Plato, who came to set a long-lasting "contemplative precedence." Its long standing is not least due to Christian thinkers' "mixing up" or contaminating Jesus' teachings with the speculative Greek metaphysic tradition, leading to

> "... the silent abandonment by scholasticism of the central political experiences in early Christianity. Since Augustine became a neo-Platonist and Thomas Aquinas a neo-Aristotelian, their political philosophies would extract from the gospels only those features which corresponded... to the Platonic dichotomy between life lived in the 'cave' of human affairs

---

26 On the intellectual relationship between Arendt and Schmitt, see also Moyn (2008); Kalyvas (2009).

and life lived in the glaring light of the truth of the 'ideas'... (Arendt 2005, 56)

The distinctiveness of the various activities of *vita activa* fades when viewed from a contemplative perspective. It is Arendt's contention that *vita activa* consists of three elementary forms of activities—labor, work, and action— each of which corresponds to a human condition. We shall focus on action. This is since forgiveness, in Arendt's conceptualization, is a mode of action. We shall therefore only very briefly note that *labor* has to do with the purely biological; with upholding life by procuring food and by other activities necessary for this (Arendt 1989, 7). *Work* reflects that humans, in addition to their natural surroundings, needs to create something unnatural, viz. what Arendt terms a *world*. Hence, unlike the life sustaining labor activities, work activities result in products and things that cannot at first glance be consumed or used (for instance a house). Like labor, however, work is characterized by necessity, as it is determined by the purpose of the activity, or in other words, "by the category of means and ends" (Arendt 1989, 236). *Action* is "the political activity par excellence" (Arendt 1989, 9). It differs from labor and work by being, not instrumental but free, and by being constitutively inter-subjective, corresponding to "the human condition of plurality, to the fact that men, not Man, live on earth and inhabit the world" (Arendt 1989, 7). Arendt defines plurality as "the presence and acting of others" (Arendt 1989, 237). The key quality of action is initiation; action is an expression of novelty and beginning.[27] Action is spontaneous and unpredictable; it "always acts unexpectedly" (Arendt 1989, 241). As a result, humans, when acting, are not able to predict the consequences of their actions. Action, therefore, unavoidably causes *trespassing*—which exactly is the fact that forgiveness addresses since forgiveness, as we have seen, is directed to agents of trespassing.

What is generally a challenge in reading Arendt—that she uses familiar words in unfamiliar ways—applies especially to her concepts of action and politics. *Action* is a technical term with specific and sharply delimited meaning. For one thing, it is by definition political and public. As the most elementary political activity, it constitutes the political. Politics, for Arendt, basically denotes acting and speaking in public. It comes into being solely

---

27 The qualities that Arendt ascribes to action reflects the concept's connection to the human condition which Arendt terms natality. For an exploration of Arendt's notion of natality and its relation to action, see e.g. Bowen-Moore (1989).

during action, when humans "gather together and 'act in concert'," and it "disappears the moment they depart" (Arendt 1989, 244). In Arendt's account, politics is not dependent on institutions or on legislatively created spaces for action (Young-Bruehl 2009, 52).[28] In this sense, politics is unmediated: it is constituted by humans "acting and speaking directly to one another" (Arendt 1989, 183). At the same time, Arendt also stresses that humans, in political relationships, need not only to be related; there must be some distance, too, between acting people. This distance is provided by the fact that action takes place not in private or intimate relationships, but in "the light of the public realm," which, as the metaphor of light indicates, is characterized by visibility (Arendt 1989, 52). Further, in relation to her insistence on plurality as the political condition, Arendt (1993, 11) maintains that a human "in singular" is apolitical: "Politics comes into being in the in-between [*in dem Zwischen-den-Menschen*] ... and establishes itself as the relationship." Hence, for politics to exist there must be a space between humans.[29]

The unpredictability of action is intensified by the fact that it "acts into" a plurality—that the action of an individual comes into being in, and becomes a part of, an already existing "web of relationships" (Arendt 1989, 184). This means that the realm of acting people is characterized by "haphazardness and moral irresponsibility" (Arendt 1989, 220). It is Arendt's remarkable claim that action cannot be judged according to moral standards, which take "into account motives and intentions on the one hand and aims and consequences on the other" (Arendt 1989, 205). Such moral criteria apply only to what Arendt calls *behavior*, which is familiar, habitual, repetitive, and predictable. Action, in turn, "can be judged only by the criterion of greatness because it is in its nature to break through the commonly accepted and reach into the extraordinary." In addition, the criterion of greatness, "or the specific meaning of each deed, can lie only in the performance itself and neither in its motivation nor its achievement" (Arendt 1989, 205f).[30]

---

28 Whether Arendt's concept of politics is inherently anti-institutional is a disputed question; see Jalustic (2011, 308–309).

29 Arendt's notion of in-between is a much more complex notion than what we can account for here. For an explanation of it, and its relation to Arendt's notion of *world*, see Yano (2011, 309ff.).

30 This reflects that action, in Arendt's definition, cannot be a means to an end—it is not determined by an idea of its end target, but is an end in itself—which is the reason why its criterion lies, solely, in its performance. That Arendt considers action to be spontaneous and contingent to such a degree that it is detached from motives as well as consequences has made critics ascribing to her a kind of "actionism,"questioning how action, then, can be judged and what actually "remains" of action (Speight 2002, 528). And as Young-Bruehl (2007, 87) remarks, Arendt declares that greatness is the only criterion of action without touching upon the otherwise obvious moral and political question of "whether there are good and bad actions, good and bad greatness."

Arendt's depiction of action is thus two-sided: while she celebrates the greatness of action, she also pays much attention to the negative consequences of action, to the dangers and costs of action, talking about the "predicament," "calamities," "frailty," "hazards," and "frustration" of action (Arendt 1989, 188–192, 195–196, 220–222, 236–237). The costs of action and the greatness of action both stem from the contingent and spontaneous character of action; they are two sides of the same coin. Historically, Arendt identifies the recognition and appreciation of the greatness and glory of action in ancient Greece; notably before Plato and outside of philosophy, namely, as Young-Bruehl (2009, 54) observes, in the writings of Presocratic poets, historians, and dramatists. These Presocratics recognized that politics is not dependent on organized or legislatively created spaces for action, or on political organization or government, but simply on people coming together, "acting in concert" (Arendt 1989, 162; Young-Bruehl 2009, 52). Whereas Arendt regarded the ancient Greeks as the first to acknowledge action, she held that "Jesus knew what action is better than anybody else" (Arendt 1973). Jesus knew not only about the greatness and glory of action; he also had striking insights into the risks and frailties of action and how these can be remedied. It is the latter which Arendt highlights in her rendition of Jesus. Above all, Arendt's Jesus contributes to Arendt's argument that "the necessary corrective for the inevitable damages resulting from action" is not to be found outside of action or outside of the realm of human affairs—it "does not arise out of another and possibly higher faculty"—but is "one of the potentialities of action itself" (Arendt 1989, 239, 236–237). This potentiality is the human "power to forgive" (Arendt 1989, 236). Forgiveness, as Arendt conceptualizes it, is thus a self-referential action in the sense that it addresses the negative consequences of action which Arendt terms *trespassing*.

As to the question of the role of Jesus in Arendt's political thought, it can be concluded that he is unique in that he acknowledged the dangers and frailties of action without being hostile to action. This was possible because of his "forgiveness discovery": that he found a remedy against the dangers of action in one of the potentials of action itself. He allowed, accordingly, for the realization of freedom and contingency inherent in action. Unlike the trend in the tradition of political thought, he did not "do violence" to the phenomenology of action; he did not try to "over-rule" or control action (for instance by way of conceptualizing action in the categories of work, as it according to

Arendt has been a common feature to do).[31] Concerning the Western tradition of political thought, Jesus thus has a "corrective function." At the same time, Jesus is paradigmatic to Arendt's alternative account of action as the "political activity par excellence" (Arendt 1989, 9).

What we see here is Jesus not as an apocalyptic or eschatological preacher, but as a worldly oriented figure who articulated a number of striking insights into the nature of human action. Yet, there are exceptions: Arendt does in fact attribute some non-political features to Jesus. In addition to what we have touched upon—centered around love—it concerns "the activity of goodness" (Arendt 1989, 74). Goodness, as "taught by Jesus in words and deeds," is an extraordinary and extreme phenomenon, insists Arendt (1989, 74). What makes it so is not least that it demands total self-forgetfulness. Whereas action is constitutively inter-subjective and an acting person "reveals" herself to other persons, the agent of a good deed is not revealed to anyone—notably not even to the agent herself; a good deed must be wholly unacknowledged and anonymous, otherwise it dissolves. That is, not only is it not inter-personal; it is not even *intra*-personal (like "the activity of thinking" which Arendt [1978, 185] famously describes as an intra-personal dialogue between "me and myself"). It is a radically lonely activity. Arendt (1989, 74) writes:

> [T]he moment a good work becomes known and public, it loses its specific character of goodness, of being done for nothing but goodness' sake. When goodness appears openly, it is no longer goodness, though it may still be useful as organized charity... Goodness can exist only when it is not perceived, not even by its author; whoever sees himself performing a good work is no longer good, but at best a useful member of society or a dutiful member of a church. Therefore: "Let not thy left hand know what thy right hand doeth."

The "curious negative quality of goodness, the lack of outward phenomenal manifestation," Arendt (1989, 74-75) argues, is the reason why Jesus "thought

---

31 Arendt maintains that Plato introduced work as the basic political concept. That work is a key concept in Plato's idealism is not obvious. Arendt's point is that Plato understood political activity instrumentally, on the basis of an idea of its *telos*. Moreover, Arendt (1989, 17) argues that the hierarchical order between active and contemplative life has been reversed in modernity, so that active life is now favored, while contemplative life tends to disappear entirely. However, notably, this has not brought along a "revaluation" of action, as work achieves "first place" amongst *vita activa*'s activities. It is Arendt's claim that the contemplative legacy, ironically, lives on in modernity in the primacy of work. One of Arendt's examples is the Marxist notion of *making* a revolution based on the idea of its end point (see Arendt 2006b).

and taught that no man can be good: 'Why callest thou me good? none is good, save one, that is, God.'" Though a good deed "appears in the space where other activities are performed… [it] is of an actively negative nature; fleeing the world and hiding from its inhabitants, it negates the space the world offers to men, and most of all that public part of it where everything and everybody are seen and heard by others" (Arendt 1989, 77). This means that forgiveness and "doing good as an activity" do not "belong into the same category," Arendt (1960a) maintains; for the interpersonal quality and "mutuality… is essential for the act of forgiving," whereas it "remains outside all consideration of 'doing good'." Furthermore, whereas Arendt sees forgiveness as a political *conditio sine qua non*, goodness is understood as a political vice. Any attempt to adapt or transfer goodness to politics is a profound and dangerous misunderstanding, stresses Arendt (2006b, 72–78).[32]

In this regard, then, goodness bears affinity to love: both must be kept strictly separate from the public and political. In relation to forgiveness, however, there is a marked difference, since love, as we have seen, is not irrelevant to forgiveness. On the contrary, love has the greatest forgiveness potential. This is due to the fact that whereas the author of a good deed is not revealed to anybody, love is eminently personal and "fully receptive to the person" (Arendt 1989, 241).

III. Arendt and the Historiography of Jesus

As briefly touched upon in the introduction, it was characteristic to the development of liberal theology in the nineteenth century to draw on Jesus as a historical person. In other words, the theological development was characterized by a shift from the supernatural Christ to Jesus as a human being. For us, three distinctive features of this development become particularly noteworthy: first, the fact that it focused on Jesus as a human being. Second, that it presented Jesus as an ethical teacher. Lastly, it is important that this development was preoccupied with pointing out the uniqueness and originality of Jesus.

The quest for the historical Jesus is a child of the Enlightenment; it is to be understood as part of the wider enlightenment project of liberating humans from traditions and institutions which were not rationally based and of disci-

---

32 In her controversial interpretation of what she saw as the failed French Revolution, Arendt connects her analysis of goodness and why it must be kept separate from politics with equally provocative accounts of compassion and pity; see Arendt (2006, 69–80). The literature on Arendt's conception of goodness is extensive; see e.g. Kateb (1984, 89–91); Canovan (1995, 175–183); Gregory (2008, 197–241).

plining human reason and conduct. Theologically, this manifested itself in a fight against church dogmas (Hallbäck 1998, 159–160). The attempt was to replace these with a rational theology connected to critical-historical inquiries. While such an approach was initiated in the Enlightenment, its heyday came in the second half of the nineteenth century.[33] What began as a rather harsh rationalism and an "underground movement" became, as Hallbäck (1998, 160) puts it, "theologically domesticated," as it became connected with a sanguine civilizing optimism: history was seen as progressive moral and civilizing process that Jesus qua his genius had anticipated.[34] Liberal theologians became concerned, in particular, with Jesus as a true, historical person. This manifested itself in the so-called "liberal lives" of Jesus, a sort of "Jesus biographies" which were highly humanistic in their flavor (Paget 2002, 144). It was a basic conviction that there was a lack of correspondence between this "true," historical Jesus and Jesus Christ as represented in the mythic and dogmatic interpretations of the church. Accordingly, in connection to the rise of modern historical method, the starting point was not the Jesus Christ of creedal orthodoxy, but examinations of the New Testament texts (Woodhead 2004, 368). The aim was to uncover the historical Jesus from behind layers of accretions of the Christian tradition and dogmas and, notably, to understand the "uncovered," true person of Jesus as a model, an ideal human whose teachings should be learned and imitated. This was interrelated to a "moralization" of theology: the uncovered paradigmatic human of Jesus was, above all, construed as an ethical teacher. This ethical focus, in combination with suspicion towards traditions, was connected to a strong anti-institutional tendency: Jesus tended to be depicted as teaching a purely ethical religion without any external elements (such as church, priests, rituals, dogmas, etc.) (Woodhead 2004, 368).

Liberal theologians thus sought a Jesus who was "explicable within the limits of human history" (Gowler 2011, 301). They sought a Jesus who was subjected to human conditions. As Heschel (1998, 17) observes, the "rejection of the super-natural left little else than the historical figure of Jesus, whose

---

33 True, a growing skepticism and doubt about the possibility of reconstructing the historical Jesus is traceable to the 1890s, but it does not become widely accepted until the twentieth century. An early skepticism can be found in the famous work by David Friedrich Strauss *Das Leben Jesu, kritisch bearbeitet* (1835–36). Few scholars, however, were as skeptical as Strauss; in general there was confidence in the possibility of uncovering Jesus as a human. See Macquarrie (1988, 30–32).

34 The Bible criticism of the enlightenment scholars was published secretly and anonymously; see Gowler (2011, 304).

greatness was derived... from his teachings and force of personality."[35] The (theological) challenge, accordingly, was to preserve the uniqueness and singularity of Jesus when described as a historical human. It was, in other words, a central concern to describe Jesus as an extraordinary and unique person and his teachings as original and unprecedented. As a result, what was singled out in these portrayals was what allegedly set Jesus apart from his surroundings. A consequence of these "de-contextualization" attempts was, as Herschel (1998) has shown, that contemporary Judaism tended to be described in negative terms. This was in order to elevate Jesus to a unique figure. The more Jesus conformed to his historical context, the less original he was.[36]

Intensive historical research, however, made the task of preserving Jesus' uniqueness increasingly difficult, as well as it raised questions about the possibility of reconstructing the historical Jesus. One challenge arose from the fact that the historical research around the turn of the century brought to light a particular aspect of Jesus' historical context: eschatological and apocalyptic Jewish ideas.[37] Yet another "theological challenge" resulting from the historical research concerns the value of the New Testament documents as sources for the historical Jesus. In 1892, Martin Kähler published a pioneering work in which he observed that the preached Christ and the Jesus of history are intermeshed in the gospels to such a degree that it is practically impossible to extract the historical facts (Kähler 2013; cf. Paget 2002, 145; Macquarrie 1988, 31). This historical skepticism was followed up by William Wrede (1901), who also argued that the gospels could not be regarded as historically reliable records of the life of Jesus; rather, they were theologically determined narratives that reflected the later community's "post-Easter" faith in Christ which was projected onto Jesus—who had not understood himself as messiah.[38] Moreover, Albert Schweitzer (1906) wrote a historiographical work on

---

35 Though liberal theologians surrendered many aspects of the supernatural, they did, however, identify (Jesus') morality with the divine. For an account of the fact that they were not "prepared to detach the sacred from morality" and of how this relates to Immanuel Kant's attempt to secure faith by distinguishing it from empirical knowledge, see Woodhead (2004, 366–370, 369).

36 Jewish theological-historical scholars, in turn, insisted on the Jewishness of Jesus and that he had taught the ethical principles of (Pharisaic) Judaism. For an exposition of this German-Jewish tradition of scholarship on Jesus which ran from Abraham Geiger (1810–74) to Martin Buber (1878-1965), see Heschel (1998).

37 Important works in this regard include Weiss (1892) and Schweitzer (1901); see Müller (2003, 367–368).

38 To be more precise, Wrede focused on the Gospel of Mark which had otherwise been identified as the oldest gospel and, hence, most reliable.

the life of Jesus research in which he pointed out the projections of the liberal-theological pictures of Jesus. These, so to speak, "human, all too human"
pictures were determined by the ethical ideals which, in the view of their
authors, were most worth trying to aspire to (Schweitzer 1906; cf. Theissen
and Merz 1998, 5–6).[39] These insights led to a dramatic change of the "Jesus
paradigm." Instead of the image of an ethical, humanistic, and worldly figure,
Jesus came to be construed as an eschatological and apocalyptical preacher
who announced the imminent end of history and the world.[40]

In the interwar period, the possibility of reconstructing the historical Jesus
was further questioned (e.g. Dibelius 1919; Schmitt 1919; Bultmann 1921).
This led to what was to become the predominant view; namely that it is methodologically impossible to reconstruct the historical Jesus.[41] Among the leading spokesmen of this view was Rudolf Bultmann, Arendt's teacher in theology at Marburg. Bultmann had begun his career as a historical-theological
scholar, but in the early 1920s he approached the so-called dialectical theological movement formed after the First World War and led by Karl Barth.[42]
Important from our perspective is it that one of its distinctive features was a
marked anti-historicism. This indicates a rejection of what historicism was
associated with, such as historical progressivism and relativism. In line with
this anti-historicist current, Bultmann argued that not only was it methodologically impossible to reconstruct the historical Jesus, it was also a theologically misguided project. Faith cannot be dependent on uncertain, relativistic
results of historical science. As faith is a matter of personal decision, it was,
theologically speaking, actually an advantage that the gospels bought witness
only to the faith of the community, not to the historical Jesus. What was decisive was not what Jesus had said and done, but what God had said and done in
the cross and resurrection (Theissen and Merz 1998, 6). In terms of sources,
this was accompanied with a shift of focus from the Synoptic Gospels (that is,
Mark, Matthew, and Luke) to Paul and St. John's Gospel (Hallbäck 1998, 162).

---

39 In fact, Kähler pointed to this projection already in 1892, stating that the liberal image of Jesus
"is just a modern variation of human inventive art, no better than the infamous dogmatic Christ of
Byzantine Christology" (Kähler 2013, 16; also quoted in Macquarrie 1988, 31). Strangely, Schweitzer
does not mention Kähler's work.

40 For thoughtful comments on the ways in which the apocalyptic and anti-idealistic Jesus-image was
in accord, too, with its time (with the *fin de siecle* culture, the growing "civilizing discontent," and the
passing of the era of the liberal *Kultur-synthese*), see Hallbäck (2008, 40ff).

41 In fact, widespread scholarly discussions of and inquiries into the historical Jesus did not re-
emerge until the 1980s.

42 The question as to how close Bultmann in this period got to Barth and the dialectical theology is a
disputed one; see Hammann 2009, 134–148.

Despite his critique of "Jesus preoccupation," Bultmann wrote a book enti-tled *Jesus*, which came out in 1926 (that is, at the time when Arendt studied with him). Yet his interpretation is not based on the historical person of Jesus. He emphasizes that he is not exploring Jesus as a religious hero or as an ideal human being. Accordingly, he points out that when he writes "Jesus," he is referring to "a complex of ideas in the oldest layer of the synoptic tradition which is the object of our consideration." Famously, he adds that "[w]hoever prefers to put the name of 'Jesus' always in quotation marks and let it stand as an abbreviation for the historical phenomenon with which we are con-cerned, is free to do so" (Bultmann 1988, 18). Needless to say, this does not change the fact that Bultmann did anyhow draw an image, be it of Jesus or of "Jesus." It also does not change the fact that, arguably, his "Jesus" is the object of projections, too, since "Jesus" is depicted very much like an ideal dialectical-existential theologian.[43] Finally, Bultmann's portrayal is "minimal-istic" in the sense that he confines himself solely to the teachings of "Jesus." What is particularly interesting from our perspective is that Bultmann's book concludes with a lengthy section on forgiveness. Bultmann's thinking on forgiveness, however, is dominated by (Lutheran) individualist notions, par-ticularly the God-self relation. In other words, he chiefly reflects on forgive-ness between God and the individual human being, rather than forgiveness between humans. Despite that Arendt held Bultmann in high regard, her interpretations of forgiveness and of Jesus are thus essentially different from Bultmann's.[44] Above all, she is critical of the shift from what Jesus had said and done to what God had said and done in the resurrection. Characterizing this as a Pauline misapprehension, Arendt (1992, 221) objects to the "con-spicuous neglect ... of Jesus' preaching as opposed to Christ as 'God's work of salvation,'" which she sees as "an exclusive regard for the functional and a pushing aside of the real 'substance.' Jesus thus remains interesting only in his function within God's work of salvation on earth, not as a 'preacher' who says: You should or should not do this or that."

The remarks on the historiography of Jesus do not to seek to demonstrate any direct link between Arendt and the tradition of liberal theology. Indeed,

---

43 Cf. Barth's dry comment on Bultmann's book: "Jesus has apparently become a dialectical theologian" (quoted in Hamman (2009, 187)).

44 Hence, in a letter to Karl Jaspers, Arendt wrote that "Bultmann is a truly great scholar" (Arendt and Jaspers 1992, 221–222). See also Hans Jonas (2008, 61) who recalls that Arendt "became a terrific student of Bultmann's... [S]he had such an intense interest in the New Testament that she spent several semesters studying with him."

Arendt differs fundamentally from this tradition on a number of points. For example, the image of Jesus as an ethical teacher and paradigmatic human was connected to notions of moral perfectibility and civilizing optimism. Also, Arendt's emphasis on the unforgivable and her references to extermination by drowning and burning are not exactly congenial to the sanguine civilizing optimism of liberal theology. It should be clear, however, that there are some parallels: the approach to Jesus as a historical person without "adding" a Christiologic interpretation; the drawing on "non-apocalyptic" parts of the Synoptic Gospels and the equating of their narratives of the "earthly Jesus" with the historical Jesus; the emphasis on the uniqueness and originality of Jesus and the portrayal of him as a genius (albeit for Arendt not a religious genius, but a purely "humanistic genius"); the focus on his ethical teaching; the perception of him as "anti-institutional," and the doubts about how his teaching has been interpreted in the Christian tradition.[45] Thus, in answer to Young-Bruehl's (2009, 61) comment that "there had been no precedent for drawing upon the thought of Jesus of Nazareth as a historical person and a political sage," this can only be the case if one assumes that there is a definite and fundamental difference between ethics and (Arendt's notion of) politics. However, what is generally the case with Arendt's political thought—that it is ethically engaged—is in particular the case with her reflections on forgiveness. Additionally, it was characteristic of Arendt to move across disciplinary boundaries. Beyond this, the comparison between Arendt and the theological enlightenment tradition is interesting in view of Arendt's well-known anti-historicism. Still, although Arendt's way of construing Jesus on a number of points actually was in line with liberal-theological modes of thought, she did not "import" its historicism. This is obvious from the fact that she did not subscribe to its notions of moral and civilizing perfectibility and, not least, that she disregarded historical reflections and reasoning in her depiction of Jesus. Here, it is worth bearing in mind that although the liberal-theological image of Jesus does not play a role in the twentieth century historical scholarship, its image of Jesus as an extraordinary human and a moral teacher has,

---

45 Also, more generally, in depicting a betrayal of primordial Christianity resulting from its institutionalization and contamination by the Greek metaphysical tradition, Arendt's narrative conforms to Protestantism.

as Hallbäck (2003, 373) points out, survived in the work of humanistic Jesus-interpreters. Arendt's Jesus appears to be a good example of this.[46]

Conclusion

The exploration of Arendt's rendition of Jesus has confirmed that an image of Jesus tends to reflect its author and her time. Thus, for several reasons, Arendt's image can be characterized as a post-Holocaust image. First, because Arendt's Jesus emphasizes the limits of forgiveness and the category of the unforgivable. Furthermore, Arendt's Jesus indicates that there are wrongdoers who are not only unforgivable, but who should be destroyed. By the same token, her Jesus is a proponent of a highly circumscribed forgiveness in as far as he "excludes" from forgiveness all sorts of deliberate wrongdoing. It seems from Arendt's descriptions of offences, however, that what she really had in mind was not merely "minor deliberate wrongdoing," but radical evil and totalitarian crimes. This testifies to the interpretation that Arendt's image of Jesus is a post-Holocaust image.

Moreover, it can be concluded that Arendt's image of Jesus was "ambivalent" or inconclusive. This is due to the paradoxical fact that while Arendt's Jesus teaches a circumscribed forgiveness, he also praises the greatness and extraordinary nature of the human power to forgive. Hence, there appears to be a discrepancy between the qualities and the addressee or scope of forgiveness.

Whereas Arendt's rendition of Jesus thus reflects post-war issues, it is noteworthy that it did not conform to the apocalyptic and eschatological image of Jesus which prevailed in the theology of her time. In this regard, her depiction had more in common with a previous "Jesus paradigm," viz. the liberal-theological image of Jesus as an ethical teacher and ideal human. As we have seen, there are several parallels between Arendt and this tradition—in particular the presentation of Jesus as a unique and extraordinary human and the connecting of this uniqueness with his ethical teachings. These similarities show that even though Arendt's drawing on Jesus in the framework of political theory was unconventional, how she did so was not as original as it might have seemed at first glance. The claim that what she did was altogether unprecedented can only be made if one assumes that there are insurmount-

---

46 Another good example of this is Karl Jaspers (1958), Arendt's doctoral supervisor, who included Jesus among his "great philosophers." As Arendt was in close correspondence with Jaspers and edited the English version of his history of philosophy, she evidently knew about his portrayal of Jesus. Yet, apart from construing Jesus as an extraordinary human and a philosopher, Arendt's and Jaspers' interpretations do not have much in common.

able boundaries between academic disciplines—but after all, Arendt was characterized by the opposite: by being distinctively inter-disciplinary.

Finally, it can be concluded that Arendt's rendition of Jesus functions as a part of her critique of the Western tradition of political thought. She uses her depiction of Jesus as one of her strategies for rectifying and rethinking the political, for bringing it into accord with her account of human conditions and experiences. However, the relationship between Arendt's Jesus and her political thought is not without ambiguity since she ascribes to Jesus some anti-political aspects too; chiefly goodness. Accordingly, Arendt's Jesus, on one hand, "taught in words and deeds" the decidedly anti-political activity of goodness, while, on the other hand, he had unique insights into action as "the political activity par excellence" and forgiveness as an indispensable, political experience (Arendt 1989, 9, 74). In either case, Arendt's image of Jesus serves her political thought insofar as it can be seen as a part of a "definition fight" over the political. Hence, unlike forgiveness, goodness has often been interpreted as having political relevance. Moreover, while Arendt contends that forgiveness should be included in political theory, she argues that goodness does not belong to the political. That Arendt associates Jesus with some phenomena which must be kept separate from politics does not then change the fact that her interpretation of Jesus serves her political thought.[47]

47 Acknowledgements: I owe a great debt of gratitude to Paul Leer-Salvesen. For their comments on parts of this essay and for discussions on issues related to it, I would also like to thank warmly Martin van Gelderen, Nicola Hargreaves, Martin Laube, Mogens Müller, Jimmi Nielsen, and Mathias Wilke.

References

Arendt, Hannah. 1960a. "Arendt letter to Auden (14 February 1960)." In *General Correspondence 1938–1976*. Hannah Arendt Papers. Manuscript Division, Library of Congress. Washington, D.C.

———. 1960b. *Vita Activa—oder Vom tätigen Leben*. Stuttgart: W. Kohlhammer.

———. 1970 [1968]. *Men in Dark Times*. London: Lowe & Brydone.

———. 1973. "Remarks at the American Society for Christian Ethics, January 21, 1973." In *The Papers of Hannah Arendt* at the Library of Congress, container 70, 01183 8-0118 39.

———. 1978. *The Life of the Mind: Two/Willing*. New York: Harcourt Brace Jovanovich.

———. 1989 [1958]. *The Human Condition*. Chicago: University of Chicago Press.

———. 1993. *Was ist Politik? Fragmente aus dem Nachlass*. Edited by Ursula Ludz. Munich: Piper.

———. 1996a. *Ich will verstehen. Selbstauskünfte zu Leben und Werk*. Edited by Ursula Ludz. Munich: Piper.

———. 1996b. *Love and Saint Augustine*. Chicago: University of Chicago Press.

———. 2003. *Responsibility and Judgment*. Edited by Jerome Kohn. New York: Schocken Books.

———. 2005. *The Promise of Politics*. Edited by Jerome Kohn. New York: Schocken Books.

———. 2006a [1961]. *Between Past and Future*. New York: Penguin Books.

———. 2006b [1963]. *On Revolution*. New York: Penguin Books.

———. 2006c [1963]. *Eichmann in Jerusalem. A Report on the Banality of Evil*. New York: Penguin Books.

———. and Karl Jaspers. 1992. *Correspondence 1926–1969*. Edited by Lotte Kohler and Hans Saner. Translated by Robert and Rita Kimber. New York: Harcourt Brace Jovanovich.

Bernauer, James, ed. 1987. *Amor Mundi. Explorations in the faith and thought of Hannah Arendt*, Boston: Springer.

Bernauer, James. 2007. "A Catholic Conversation with Hannah Arendt." In *Friends on the Way: Jesuits Encounter Contemporary Judaism*, edited by Thomas Michel, 142–165. New York: Fordham University Press.

Bernstein, Richard. 1996. *Hannah Arendt and the Jewish Question*. Cambridge: MIT Press.

Bowen-Moore, Patricia. 1989. *Hannah Arendt's Philosophy of Natality*. New York: St. Martin's Press.

Bultmann, Rudolf. 1921. *Die Geschichte der synoptischen Tradition*. Göttingen: Vandenhoeck & Ruprecht.

———. 1988 [1926]. *Jesus*. Tübingen: Mohr Siebeck.

Cannovan, Margaret. 1995 [1992]. *Hannah Arendt: A Reinterpretation of Her Political Thought*.

Cambridge: Cambridge University Press. 2011. Edited by Ian A. McFarland, David A. S. Fergusson, Karen Kilby, Iain R. Torrance.

Christophersen, Alf and Claudia Schulze. 2002. "Hannah Arendt—Paul Tillich. Briefwechsel." *Zeitschrift für Neuere Theologiegeschichte (Journal for the History of Modern Theology)* 9: 131–156.

Colle, Ralph Del. 2011. "Mortal Sin" and "Venial Sin." In *The Cambridge Dictionary of Christian Theology*, 325, 529. New York: Cambridge University Press.

Dibelius, Martin. 1919. *Die Formgeschichte des Evangeliums*. Tübingen: Mohr Siebeck.

Dürr, Thomas. 2009. *Hannah Arendt's Begriff des Verzeihens*. Freiburg and Munich: Verlag Karl Alber.

Furnish, Victor Paul. 1965. *The Jesus-Paul Debate: From Baur to Bultmann*. Manchester: Manchester University Press.

Gordon, Peter Eli. 2007. "The Concept of the Apolitical: German Jewish Thought and Weimar Political Theology." *Social Research* 74: 855–878.

Gottlieb, Susannah Young-ah. 2003. *Regions of Sorrow: Anxiety and Messianism in Hannah Arendt and W. H. Auden*. Stanford: Stanford University Press.

Gowler, David B. 2011. "The Quest for the Historical Jesus: An Overview." In *The Blackwell companion to Jesus*, edited by Delbert Burkett, 301–319. Singapore: Wiley-Blackwell.

Gregory, Eric. 2008. *Politics & the Order of Love: An Augustinian Ethic of Democratic Citizenship*. Chicago: University of Chicago Press.

Hagedorn, Ludger. 2007. "Verzeihen und Versprechen als ,Mächte' politischen Handelns? Ansätze bei Hannah Arendt." In *Lebenswelt und Politik. Perspektiven der Phänomenologie nach Husserl*, edited by Giovanni Leghissa and Michael Staudigl, 275–292. Würzburg : Königshausen & Neumann.

Hammann, Konrad. 2009. *Rudolf Bultmann. Eine Biographie*. Tübingen: Mohr Siebeck.

Hallbäck, Geert. 1998. "Den historiske Jesus som teologisk project – en kritisk betragtning." In *Den historiske Jesus og hans betydning*, edited by Troels Engberg-Pedersen, 159–177. Copenhagen: Gyldendal.

———. 2003 (1998). "Dom, dommedag" and "Jesus." In *Gads Bibelleksikon*, edited by H. J. Lundager Jensen and Geert Hallbäck, 136–137 and 369–374. Copenhagen: Gads Forlag.

———. 2008. Fra apokalyptiker til vismand." In Geert Halbäck: *Hvad jeg skrev: udvalgte artikler om Det Nye Testamente og andre ting*, 39–55. Copenhagen: Anis.

Heschel, Susannah. 1998. *Abraham Geiger and the Jewish Jesus*. Chicago: University of Chicago Press.

Jalusic, Vlasta. 2011. "Politik." In *Arendt-Handbuch. Leben—Wek—Wirkung*, edited by Wolfgang Heuer, Bernd Heiter, and Stefanie Rosenmüller, 308–309. Stuttgart and Weimar: Verlag J. B. Metzler.

Jaspers, Karl, and Rudolf Bultmann. 1954. *Die Frage der Entmythologisierung*. Munich: Piper.

Jonas, Hans. 2008. *Memoirs*. Edited by Christian Wiese. Translated by Krishna Winston. Hannover and London: Brandeis University Press.

Kalyvas, Andreas. 2009. *Democracy and the Politics of the Extraordinary: Max Weber, Carl Schmitt, and Hannah Arendt*. Cambridge: Cambridge University Press.

Kateb, George. 1984. *Hannah Arendt: Politics, Conscience, Evil*. Oxford: Martin Robertson & Company Ltd.

Kähler, Martin. 2013 [1892]. *Der sogenannte historische Jesus und der geschichtliche, biblische Christus*. Berlin: Berlin University Press.

Levinas, Emmanuel. 1990. *Nine Talmudic Readings*. Translated by Annette Aronowicz. Bloomington and Indianapolis: Indiana University Press.

Macquarrie, John. 1988. "Die Suche nach dem historischen Jesus und ihre Kritik." In *Theologische Realenzyklopädie*, vol. 17, edited by Gerhard Krause, 30–32. Berlin: Walter de Gruyter

Malcolm, Lois. 2010. "Forgiveness as New Creation: Christ and the Moral Life Revisited." In *Christology and Ethics*, edited by LeRon Shults and Brent Waters, 99–127. Michigan: Wm. B. Eerdmans Publishing Co.

Moyn, Samuel. 2008. "Hannah Arendt on the Secular." *New German Critique* 35: 71–96.

Müller, Mogens. 2003. "Jesu-liv-forskningen." In *Gads Bibelleksikon*, edited by H. J. Lundager Jensen and Geert Hallbäck, 367–368. Copenhagen: Gads Forlag.

Nietzsche, Friedrich. 2013 [1889]. *Der Antichrist: Fluch auf das Christentum*. Berlin: Create Space Independent Publishing Platform.

Paget, James Carleton. 2002. "Quests for the historical Jesus." In *Cambridge Companion to Jesus*, edited by Markus Bockmuehl, 138–156. Port Chester, NY: Cambridge University Press.

Pullich, Leif. 1999. "Hannah Arendt über das Verzeihen." *Journal Phänome-nologie* 11: 4–12.

Schmitt, Carl. 2004 [1922]. *Political Theology: Four Chapters on the Concept of Sovereignty.*

Translated by George D. Schwab. Chicago: University of Chicago Press.

Schmidt, Karl Ludwig. 1919. *Der Rahmen der Geschichte Jesu: literarturkritische Untersuchungen zur ältesten Jesusüberlieferung.* Berlin: Trowitzsch & Sohn.

Schanz, Hans-Jørgen. 2004. "En kristen tænker?—om Hannah Arendt." In *Modernitet og kapitalisme,* 119–135. Aarhus: Forlaget Modtryk.

———. 2007. *Handling og ondskab: en bog om Hannah Arendt.* Aarhus: Aarhus University Press.

Scheiber, Karin. 2006. *Vergebung: eine systematisch-theologische Untersuchung.* Tübingen: Mohr Siebeck.

Schweitzer, Albert. 1901 [1956]. *Das Messianitäts- und Leidensgeheimnis—eine Skizze des Lebens Jesu.* Tübingen: J. C. B. Mohr.

———. 1906. *Von Reimarus Zu Wrede: Eine Geschichte Der Leben-Jesu-Forschung.* Tübingen: Mohr Siebeck.

———. 1984 [1913]. *Geschichte der Leben-Jesu-Forschung.* Stuttgart: Mohr Sie-beck.

Speight, Allen. 2002. "Arendt and Hegel on the tragic nature of action." *Philosophy & Social Criticism* 28: 523–536.

Theissen, Gerd, and Annette Merz. 1998. *The historical Jesus: A comprehensive guide.* Translated by John Bowden. Minneapolis: Fortress Press.

Villa, Dana R. 1996. *Arendt and Heidegger: The Fate of the Political.* Princeton: Princeton University Press.

Waters, Brent. 2010. "The Incarnation and the Christian Moral Life." In *Christology and Ethics,* edited by LeRon Shults and Brent Waters, 5–32. Michigan: Wm. B. Eerdmans Publishing Co.

Weigel, Sigrid. 2002. "Secularization and Sacralization, Normalization and Rupture: Kristeva and Arendt on Forgiveness." *Publications of the Modern Language Association of America* 117: 320–323.

Weiss, Johannes. 1964 [1892]. *Die Predigt von Jesu vom Reiche Gottes.* Göttingen: Vandenhoeck & Ruprecht.

Wolterstorff, Nicholas. 2008. "Jesus and Forgiveness." In *Jesus and Philosophy. New Essays,* edited by Paul K. Moser, 194–214. Cambridge: Cambridge University Press.

Woodhead, Linda. 2004. *An Introduction to Christianity.* Cambridge: Cambridge University Press.

Wrede, William. 1901. *Das Messiasgeheimnis in den Evangelien. Zugleich ein Beitrag zum Verständnis des Markusevangeliums.* Göttingen: Vandenhoeck & Ruprecht.

Yano, Kumiko. 2011. "Politischer Raum/ 'Zwischen'." In *Arendt-Handbuch. Leben—Wek—Wirkung,* edited by Wolfgang Heuer, Bernd Heiter, and Stefanie Rosenmüller, 309–311. Stuttgart and Weimar: Verlag J. B. Metzler.

Young-Bruehl, Elisabeth. 2006. *Why Arendt Matters.* New Haven: Yale University Press.

———. 2009. "Hannah Arendt on forgiveness." In *Considering Forgiveness,* edited by Aleksandra Wagner and Carin Kuoni, 48–64. New York: Vera List Center for Art and Politics.

www.ingramcontent.com/pod-product-compliance
Lightning Source LLC
Chambersburg PA
CBHW020327130626
46549CB00003B/1054